# BERKSHIRE
# TALES OF MYSTERY
# AND MURDER

# BERKSHIRE TALES OF MYSTERY AND MURDER

David Kidd-Hewitt

COUNTRYSIDE BOOKS
NEWBURY BERKSHIRE

COUNTRYSIDE BOOKS
3 Catherine Road
Newbury, Berkshire

To view our complete range of books,
please visit us at
www.countrysidebooks.co.uk

ISBN 1 85306 880 2

*To my family*

Produced through MRM Associates Ltd., Reading
Printed by Cromwell Press, Trowbridge

# Contents

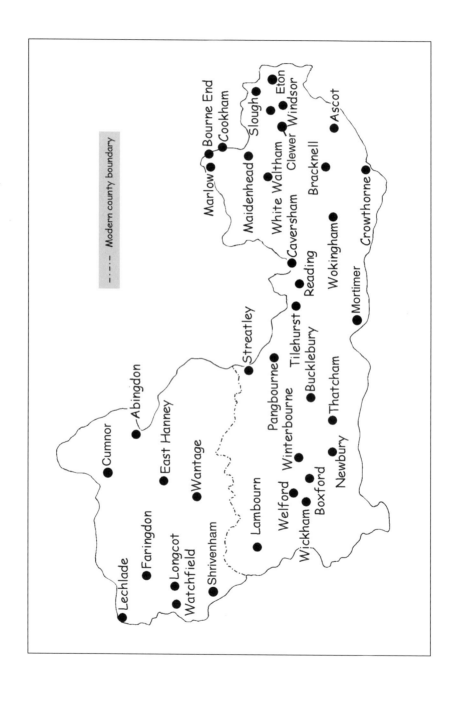

- - - - - Modern county boundary

Lechlade
Faringdon
Longcot
Watchfield
Shrivenham
Cumnor
Abingdon
East Hanney
Wantage
Lambourn
Welford
Winterbourne
Wickham
Boxford
Newbury
Thatcham
Pangbourne
Streatley
Tilehurst
Bucklebury
Caversham
Reading
Mortimer
Wokingham
Crowthorne
Marlow
Bourne End
Cookham
Maidenhead
Slough
White Waltham
Clewer
Windsor
Eton
Bracknell
Ascot

# FOREWORD

Writing this book has drawn me into researching some Berkshire murders and mysteries that a fiction writer would be hard-pressed to imagine, but these are fact – they actually happened. Court records, contemporary media reports and a wealth of parish and county records corroborate acts of human behaviour that defy belief. These stories include the almost casual decapitation of an innocent landlady by her lodger at Wantage; the inhuman behaviour of that victim's mother in making money from displaying her daughter's headless body; and the equally horrendous murder of a young carefree child by her father at Clewer because she 'annoyed' him. Add to these a serial wife killer from Watchfield, who managed to murder all of his children's three mothers, and a faithless Maidenhead man who callously disposed of his lover and mother to his child, giving away her possessions to a prostitute for his selfish pleasure. Who murdered Alfred Oliver of Reading? This is still on the records of unsolved county murders, so take on some detective work with the clues running through this fascinating tale; you may discover the key to this murder mystery.

Mystery and magic are brought together with a real wizard tale. It connects directly into the world of Harry Potter, but this is not fiction and neither were the powers of the black arts fought by one Wizard Palmer of Boxford. Spontaneous human combustion is a terrifying thought and for one Berkshire mother it took her life.

Other Berkshire residents were plagued by a poltergeist that literally ripped clothes, stole shoes and smashed furniture – check the poltergeist chart for clues to your haunting fears. Who was hidden in a belfry at Thatcham. Was it murder? Add the mystery of the man to tried to kill a king at Ascot; another trying to destroy his home village of Lambourn; a disastrous fight for honour at Eton; and a trip through time at Cookham, and you have a true journey of real mystery and murder ahead.

I hope you enjoy it.

David Kidd-Hewitt

# Acknowledgements

Researching true tales of mystery and murder requires a lot of digging and sifting through a variety of archives and records, and many thanks are due to all those who enthusiastically assisted my digging. Thanks go to: Elizabeth and Lee at the University of London Library's Historical Collection; the Book Delivery Staff and Jane Welsh at the British Library Newspapers at Colindale; the staff at the Berkshire Record Office; Richard Heaton; Ken Wells, Curator at the Thames Valley Police Museum, Sulhamstead; Peter Stallwood; Welford and Wickham School; Kit Withers; Shan Mills; Susan Meyer; Richard Halliwell, Curator of the Vale and Downland Museum; Peter Allen of the Thatcham Historical Society; Luke Over; Mike Hippisley Matthews; Mike Smith; Bruce James; James Black; Jeff Blackburn; the Rev. Peter Downham; Janet Bord of the Fortean Picture Library.

Finally, an overdue acknowledgement to Michael Clare, PC doctor, who kept my ancient computer going throughout the project, and to my family for their support.

# THE DIABOLICAL MURDER
# OF ANN PULLIN

'Give ear ye tender Christians all, and listen unto me,
While I relate a deed of blood, and great barbarity;
A murder of the blackest dye I now repeat in rhyme,
That was committed by George King, a young man in his prime.'

*The Trial and Confession of Geo:King*, G. Smeeton, 1834

Wantage, in old Berkshire, was the location of this 'deed of blood, and great barbarity', and it can be said, without exaggeration, to be a most horrific tale of murder of an innocent victim. It is also a tale of outrageous behaviour by the victim's family in exploiting such a terrible family tragedy. But first, let's meet the perpetrator, George King, aged 19, a native of Cumnor, also in 'old' Berkshire. His job as a itinerant fruit picker, bean and pea reaper took him to work in Court Hill Farm, just outside Wantage.

It was Friday, 30th August, 1833. Around 7 pm that evening he finished the arduous task of bean-cutting. This entailed a skilful severing of the bean stalks with a razor-sharp hooked blade, and King was fast and accurate, harvesting the beans without damage to the long, tender crops to the satisfaction of the foreman, John Heath. It was lonely, tiring, and thirsty work.

On his walk back to Wantage, King decided to stop off at the Squirrel public house in Grove Street for a well-earned beer. Then it was on to his lodgings at the White Hart in nearby Newbury

Street. This was the home of 40-year-old Mrs Ann Pullin, who lived with her six-year-old daughter and 12-year-old stepson. It was a neat house, set slightly back from the street, with a small garden and comfortable accommodation for the occasional traveller and casual farm worker such as King.

The pub was quiet that rainy evening: one man had left almost as King arrived, and another sat supping his beer, his dog by his side. Ann Pullin was a widow, and the man with the dog had taken a shine to her and had been engaged in a little courtship when he was interrupted by King's return and his request for food and beer. He decided to leave now that King was back for the evening, and so it was George King was left alone with Ann Pullin.

His kindly landlady cut him a rasher of bacon which he frizzled on the point of his knife by the log fire whilst she poured him another ale. All in all, a peaceful scene on a rainy night at the end of August, and there it might have ended, but what was to happen next was sudden and startling.

After his supper, King went out to use the toilet in the yard, and, on his return, Mrs Pullin went over and bolted the door shut for the night. In the cosy, warm security of her small pub, her two children asleep upstairs, Ann Pullin felt no need to be wary of her hard-working lodger. But how wrong can you be?

Whether it was on the spur of the moment or had been planned for some time is not known, but King decided he needed money, and the widow had what he wanted. Warmed, fed, and refreshed, King took his curved bladed bean cutter, raised it high for the last time that day, and in a moment sliced Anne Pullin's head clean off her body. With his knife, fresh from cooking the bacon the kindly woman had given him not many moments before, he then cut off her apron pocket containing her purse, and freed the pub keys from her belt. His confidence left him as he struggled with the keys in an attempt to unlock the door. In his panic, the candle dropped out of its holder and he trod on it, rendering it useless. As he fumbled in the dark, it was some little time before he could find the bolt. At last he wrenched open the door and stumbled down the steps into the street, clutching the severed pocket, keys, and the ferocious murder weapon dripping with Ann Pullin's blood.

The scene he left behind was horrific. The decapitated body of Ann Pullin lay in a crimson pool of blood, her head lying some four feet away staring sightlessly toward the doorway through which King had fled. The *Berkshire Chronicle* was later to describe the walls and floor as being covered in blood; so it would seem likely that King would also have the blood of his innocent victim on his clothes and possibly on his face and hands as he made his escape that rainy Friday night.

It was this sight that was to greet Ann's 12-year-old son James in the kitchen parlour the next morning. Calling out for his mother, he entered the kitchen some time around six or seven o'clock, excited about the prospect of a day's fishing with his friend Thomas Gregory, the milk boy. One cannot imagine the horror that confronted that young boy to see his mother's decapitated body and then her head, lying some distance away, the face of his mother frozen in the agony of death, her life blood now turned to crimson stains on the floors and walls of the kitchen.

At that moment, his friend Tom was coming up the pub steps. The door was open from King's escape the previous night, so he went in. He and James stood together as statues, transfixed by a sight that would never leave their memories. The lifeless gaze of James's mother, her crisp white bonnet, still tied under her chin in a bow, with just a trickle of blood running down her cheek, added to the horror and the feeling that at any moment she might cry out in anguish. Then the friends fled the scene to fetch help.

But what of George King? He had deserted his lodgings; so it would not be long before he was sought for questioning. What happened to him that rainy night after he had slaughtered his landlady, with – according to the *Reading Mercury* – 'as much smoothness as could possibly be effected by a Turkish scimitar'?

He had rushed out in a panic and set off towards Falcon Corner, tossing the stolen keys aside as he did so. He'd taken the widow's purse from the severed apron pocket, discarding the torn cloth in the village pond, and then headed up towards the churchyard. Some 15 or 20 minutes after leaving Newbury Street, he returned – not to the scene of his crime, the White Hart,  but to the Blue Boar, another public house, almost opposite.

Was a plan formulating in his mind to brazen it out, to play the innocent labourer going for a drink before returning to his lodgings, and then discovering his poor landlady murdered? He would often drink elsewhere before returning home, at the

Squirrel or the Sparrow, where he had a bar tab; so this was not behaviour that was out of character.

It was around 9.45 pm when George King entered the Blue Boar. The first thing that the landlord noticed when King entered was that, despite heavy rain, he had his coat doubled up on his arm. Why would you carry your coat on such a night? It would certainly be a useful way to hide a bloodstained waistcoat or perhaps a coat sleeve. It seems that King's mind was working overtime to construct an alibi. Whether his decision to go to the Blue Boar was spontaneous or pre-planned is difficult to tell. One thing common to almost all violent murders is the unexpected emotional turmoil that actually committing the crime triggers in the perpetrator, the unforeseen jittery behaviour and seemingly confused manner. Trying too hard to act normally can draw attention.

King went up to the bar and ordered a pint of beer, spilling cash onto the bar, from which he paid a halfpenny. William Betteridge, the landlord, noticed that, despite carrying his coat over his arm, he was not very wet. He obviously had not been outside long enough to be soaked to the skin, or had possibly taken his coat off just prior to entering the pub. Great observers, landlords. King was still carrying his bean hook and also, according to the landlord, a hooked stick. King did not drink the beer, but asked if he could have a bed for the night. By this time the landlady had appeared to take a look at their new customer. She saw a young man with a strong, sinewy frame. He was short, around five feet two inches tall. He had a rather forbidding, sullen look; his eyes were small and sunken; and his ears projected very noticeably. He was not an endearing sight, and she told him no, but it was likely he could get one at Mrs Pullin's opposite, at the White Hart. King fell silent; he had not expected to hear his victim's name coming back to haunt him so soon. He took his beer over to some others drinking at a nearby table and bade them have it; he no longer wanted it. If he'd wanted to act normally, he was not doing a very convincing job, giving away his freshly drawn beer to strangers only minutes after arriving. Perhaps he realized this was a foolish move, because he then offered to play anyone in the room at a game of skittles. Was this another attempt to persuade himself he could survive his murderous deed and ingratiate himself with the pub regulars, perhaps playing for time to further develop an alibi?

Without the forensic skills we use today and without the precise time of death that contemporary medical investigations are able to provide, it was much more difficult to accurately connect a suspect to the victim and the crime unless the deed had been witnessed or the suspect was found to be in possession of goods stolen from the scene of the crime. Even bloodstains could be explained as rabbit blood acquired whilst poaching or as a result of an accident whilst harvesting.

We know King had Ann Pullin's money on his person, but, if he kept it well hidden and stayed in the pub until closing time, he might still claim innocence when Mrs Pullin was discovered. He could even say that he had not yet been back to his lodgings – too busy visiting pubs and playing skittles. The landlord, though, wanted to close shortly and refused to allow skittles to be played at that time of night. It was now approaching 10.15 pm. There were approximately five other customers in the pub at that time, all witnesses to King's restless behaviour.

One was a young French lad called Charles Marriot, who was working as a bellows boy with a local blacksmith called Frampton. He was sitting alone when suddenly King went over to his table and struck up a conversation. He had an unusual proposition for him. Claiming that he was without shelter for the night, he said he hoped to find somewhere to stay at Hanney, around four miles north of Wantage, where he had been working at Court Farm. He offered to pay the French lad one shilling for his companionship on the journey. King was a desperate man; he also carried a fearsome weapon in the shape of his bean hook, so it was not surprising that Marriot said no to this suggestion. King then asked if Marriot would help him find another tavern to lodge at, and this time Marriot agreed. They set off into the rainy night.

The White Hart opposite was in darkness, a black shroud hiding its gruesome secret from the innocent Marriot. How King must have hurried him past, onto other Wantage taverns to try their luck. But it wasn't to be: all were closed or closing and not available to last minute lodgers. Further pleading by King, a strange admission that he was frightened of being alone in the dark, plus the promise of money led Marriot to reveal his own resting place in a nearby stable in Back Street. King agreed to pay Marriot sixpence to stay with him.

The pub, where George King met Charles Marriott, is still a flourishing inn today.

After a night of restless mumbling and thrashing about, including a threat to hang himself, which kept Marriot awake, King was on his way by early light, telling Marriot that he was off to Hanney. Marriot was relieved to see his unwelcome guest leave and later described him as being 'all in a fidget'.

Whilst the headless body of Ann Pullin lay in a bloody mess on her kitchen floor, her children, now orphans, still asleep in their beds, King had already been wielding his lethal bean hook up at Court Farm that bright Saturday morning. Indeed, King had noticed it had blood on the blade as he started his work. The candlelight in the pub had not revealed this tell-tale clue, but the early morning light clearly showed the stain of his murderous deed of the previous night. The morning dew soon cleaned it, though, and he also washed in a nearby river and secreted his coat under a bean sheaf.

Meanwhile, back at the White Hart, James and his friend Tom had run to fetch family and friends, who in turn alerted the police and the Wantage surgeon, Henry Osmond. Word spread around the neighbourhood about the terrible beheading of Ann Pullin. Villagers jostled to see the site of the slaying, whilst Police Constable Thomas Jackson did his best to keep them from interfering with the crime scene.

It was now about 7.45 am on Saturday, 31st August, as Dr Henry Osmond examined Ann Pullin's body. He was in no doubt that the beheading had been caused by a single powerful blow from a sharp blade, severing it at the second vertebra. He could not see any notches on the bone that would indicate several blows being made to part the head from the body, as might result from using a wood axe or kitchen knife, for example. This had been carried out with a finely-honed blade such as a pea- or bean-hook, able to cut cleanly through the bone. He also noted that the deceased had a very small neck so that it would not have required much force to sever the head from the body, merely a very sharp instrument and a blow at the correct angle.

The coroner, Edward Cowcher, arrived at midday, having been busy calling together a jury for an immediate inquest into Mrs Pullin's death. Together with the county magistrate, Thomas Goodlake, they viewed the body and spoke with Dr Osmond. It did not take long for the finger to point at George King, who had in fact been seen by young Tom Gregory entering his friend's house, the White Hart, at around 9 pm the previous night. Others could confirm that around 30 to 40 minutes later he was in the Blue Boar, in an agitated state and carrying a bean hook.

In fact, two men were implicated, George King and Charles Marriot, both having been seen setting off together late the previous night from the Blue Boar.

Things started to move fast: two local labourers were sworn in to assist the coroner and set off towards the village of Hanney and Court Farm. They located the foreman, John Heath, who accompanied them to the bottom field. There was King, slicing the beans from the rows as if nothing was wrong, nothing had changed – just an honest farm labourer at work on a Saturday morning. It was now around 8.30 am. Thomas Crane, one of the labourers sworn into service by Mr Goodlake, told King they had come to arrest him and take him back to Mr Goodlake's. King did not desist. When they got there, it was noticed that he had no coat. Crane asked him if he had a coat and King said he hadn't. Asked again where his great coat was, as it was known that he had one, King admitted it was secreted under a bean sheaf in the field where he had been working and he would fetch it. It was worth a try, but King was securely detained whilst Thomas Crane was sent to find it.

Then, in the presence of the examining magistrate, Thomas Crane, Crane's father, and John Heath searched King's coat. It was damning evidence against him. It was bloodstained and the pocket contained a women's purse holding money to the value of twelve shillings, together with a bent old silver sixpenny piece. If possession of a woman's purse was not implication enough of his involvement in Ann Pullin's murder, the crooked sixpence held a significance way beyond its monetary value. Little did King know that this was not just any old sixpence, which he had attempted in vain to straighten, possibly to give to Marriot, but Ann Pullin's precious lucky sixpence, from which she was never parted. Here it was, lying on the magistrate's desk, shouting 'Murderer!' to those who knew its story. It would have to wait for Ann's friends Rachael Sandford and Eliza Clench to give it its voice and for King to realize its powerful but silent testimony against him.

King was formally arrested by PC James Jones and taken into police custody. During the afternoon, it was Marriot's turn to be apprehended as a murder suspect.

A great deal of circumstantial evidence began to build up during the inquiry as testimony was received from those, including Ann Pullin's stepson, James, who knew King was lodging at the White Hart. William Betteridge, landlord of the Blue Boar, was able to explain the meeting between Marriot and King and confirm that they were not partners in crime as far as he was aware. Marriot, himself explained how King offered him sixpence to stay with him in a stable on the night of the murder, and said that he 'appeared to be in a fidget and said he was going to hang himself'.

King was in a corner and he fought back. He told the inquest that he knew who did the murder. He had gone to the White Hart with a man called Edward Grant, who went in and 'struck off the old woman's head by a single blow'. He went on to describe her falling and the spouting of the blood, and provided an accurate description of the position of the body and the severed head. He said he had been standing by the door and was not involved in the murder at all. It was all by the hand of Grant, who had been working with him and who came from Reading.

Why King felt this would help his case is difficult to fathom. It was clearly a panic delaying tactic, but it was taken seriously by the magistrate, who dispatched messengers to try to locate the man. By Sunday morning, when it was clear that no one called Edward Grant was known in the area, King was struggling to explain away his possession of Ann Pullin's purse and, more significantly, his ownership of her lucky sixpence, identified as such by Wantage washerwoman Rachael Sandford and her friend Eliza Clench. He also had blood on his clothes, and many witnesses had testified to his irrational behaviour on the night of the murder.

As the inquest progressed into Sunday, King became more and more implicated and Marriot less and less so. Other events, difficult to believe, were taking place back at the White Hart, where Ann Pullin still lay in her dreadful state. Whilst the coroner, Edward Coucher, together with Dr Ormond, County Magistrate Thomas Goodyear, and local citizens sworn to jury service worked tirelessly to resolve this brutal murder and complete the essential legal preliminaries for a murder trial, Ann Pullin's mother had other ideas. Far from mourning the loss of her daughter in the most extreme and brutal circumstances, she and other relatives set about organizing sightseers into a paying queue. For the price of a pint of beer, they could walk past the grizzly scene, taking in the spectacle of Ann Pullin's severed head and rigid body, and the pools of dried blood. They could pass as close as possible, through the back kitchen into the street. It was a peep-show for ghouls, and they came late into the night.

Meanwhile, the inquest continued, and by Monday morning, 2nd September, King, having given up his story about Grant, was now trying to pull Marriot back into the frame, but it was too late for another red herring. The jury had no doubt that Marriot was an innocent caught up in the investigation of a murder he knew nothing about. At 2 pm on Monday, the inquest jury returned a unanimous verdict of 'wilful murder' against George King and him alone, and he was committed for trial at the next Reading Assizes, which would not be until the end of February the following year. Until then, he would languish in Reading gaol.

Now the inquest was over, Ann Pullin could be buried. However, the disgusting money-making peep-show organized by the murdered woman's own mother and certain other family members continued even when Ann was placed in her coffin. The gap between Ann's neck and her severed head had been left visible, so that paying customers could still satisfy their morbid curiosity as they filed past her open coffin. Also, as Ann was not to be buried until 2 pm the following day, the prospect of even more profit seemed to be of greater comfort to her mother than any condolences that Rachael, Eliza and other of Ann's friends could offer her for the tragic loss of her daughter. The *Berkshire Chronicle* and *Bucks Windsor Herald* for that week were incandescent with rage at the family's behaviour, calling the mother and relatives 'utterly callous to all sense of decency'. They called for the local public to condemn such behaviour.

Meanwhile, the spectators and others left their morbid peep-show to jeer at George King that Monday afternoon as he was placed into the police cart for transportation to Reading gaol. Although it seems clear that the outcome of the coming trial would be a forgone conclusion, this tale has yet another unexpected ingredient to relate, that occurred on the way to his incarceration.

# The Trial & Confession of Geo: King

## For the Diabolical Murder of Ann Pullen,

### LANDLADY OF THE WHITE HART, WANTAGE,

## BY CUTTING OFF HER HEAD with a BEAN-HOOK,

### AND WHO WAS ORDERED FOR

# EXECUTION

### MONDAY, MARCH 3, 1834.

"Thou shalt do no murder." Matthew, ch. xix. v. 18.

"Whoso sheddeth man's blood, by man shall his blood be shed." Genesis, ch. ix. v. 6.

THE trial of the above wretched man took place at Reading, on Thursday, Feb. 27, 1834, before Mr. Justice Patterson. The prisoner appeared a very heavy-looking, clumsy young man; and displayed a perfect indifference when placed at the bar.

It appeared that the deceased was a widow, living in Wantage, where she kept the White Hart Public House; her family consisting of two children, the eldest of them 12 years old.

On the 30th of August last, the eldest child, a boy, was sent to bed about nine o'clock; and, on the next morning, when he got up, he found the headless body of his mother extended on the floor with the detached head lying near the feet. He immediately called for assistance, and the prisoner was suspected, and taken into custody, and on his being searched, 12s.6d was found in his pocket, and a purse. Among the silver was a sixpence bent in a curious way, which had belonged to the deceased. The prisoner, at the inquest said, that himself and a man named Grant, had gone to the old woman's house, and that Grant went in and struck off the old woman's head by a single blow, and he described her falling, and the spouting of the blood, and the position of the body, just as was the fact, and he said that he stood at the door. Search was made for Grant, but no such person could be found. The Jury returned a verdict of Wilful Murder against the prisoner. To prove

### The Confession,

Thomas Jackson was called. He said—I took the prisoner to the Reading Goal: when we got as far as Streatly, we stopped to bait our horse at the Bull. The prisoner went up to a picture that was there, and he smiled. He said, "she

turned her eyes about like that picture, when her head was off," and he turned his own eyes like it. The prisoner joked a good deal about it while our horse was feeding. He said he had done the murder. He said he went to Mrs. Pullen's, and as he was going in doors, there was a man coming out, and another man inside the house drinking, who had a little dog, and seem'd as if he was courting the widow; he drank his beer and went away. The prisoner further said, that Mrs. Pullen cut him a rasher of bacon, which he frizzled on the point of his knife—and after having finished his supper he sat down near the window, his bean-hook and cup being on the table, and that he took up the cup in one hand and the hook in the other, and he hit her with the bean-hook, and cut her head off in a moment. He said he meant to have hit her with the back of the hook; and he said as soon as he had given the blow he fell back against the parlour door, as if some one had lifted him; but he sprang forward again and tore her pocket off, and then took the candle to get out, but could not find the bolt of the door, as he let the candle fall and trod upon it; however, on touching the bolt with his thumb, he got out, and folded the pocket up under his right arm. He said that he washed his hands in the river, and threw the pocket into a pond. I asked him how long it was all about; and he said from a quarter of an hour to 20 minutes I asked him if there was any blood about him, and he said he never thought to look, but that there was a little on the hook when he began to work the next morning, but the dew very soon washed it off.

James Jones the younger said—I was with the last witness. The prisoner said that he frizzled a rasher of bacon on his

knife, and proposed to Mrs. Pullen to pass the night with her, whereupon she said she would give him a knock on the head with a poker. That he then left the house for a short time, and on his return, he took up his bean-hook, and had her head off momentarily. He said t was not much of a blow.

The Jury immediately returned a verdict of Guilty.

Mr. Justice Patteson, in a solemn manner, passed sentence of death upon the prisoner, and ordered him for execution.

On Monday, March 3, he suffered his dreadful sentence: owing to the shortness of fall, he struggled violently some minutes, then gave a convulsive shudder, and died. He was a native of Cumnor, Oxfordshire, and was 19, the day of execution. His body was placed in a hole in one of the spare wards of the prison, without the least ceremony.

### COPY of VERSES.

GIVE ear ye tender Christians all, and listen unto me,
While I relate a deed of blood, and great barbarity;
A murder of the blackest dye I now repeat in rhyme,
That was committed by George King, a young man in his prime.

'Twas on a Friday evening, he called at the White Hart,
And there he eat and drank, until it was quite dark,
Altho' the worthy landlady did treat him very kind,
To rob and murder her, he meant wickedly design'd.

'Twas then he took his bean-hook, and with a dreadful oath,
He sever'd the head from her body with one fearful stroke,
He rifled then her pockets, and took all it did contain,
From off the ghastly body which he'd so vilely slain.

O then his guilty conscience most bitterly did him haunt,
And suspicion falling on him, he was to justice brought,
And then he stood his trial, and by the laws decree
This morning he'll die in scorn upon the fatal tree.

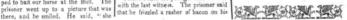

A London publisher's account of King's confession and the whole story told in verse [G. Smeeton, 1834]. (Note mis-spelling of Pullin.)

PC Thomas Jackson stopped the cart at the Bull public house at Streatley to water the horse and for PC James Jones, King, and himself to obtain refreshments. King was drawn to a picture hanging just inside the pub, and, with a strange smile, turned to PC Jackson and said, 'She turned her eyes about like that picture, when her head was off.' King could not shake off the image of her eyes following him wherever he moved.

Whilst the horse was still feeding, he began his confession to Jackson. He adopted a strange mixture of joking and despair as he recounted his fatal attack on Ann Pullin. He recalled how he had meant to hit her with the back of the hook and he said that as soon as he had given the blow, he fell back against the parlour door, as if someone had lifted him. He recalled how Mrs Pullin's eyes, after a rapid quivering, appeared to fix on him. Her head had rolled towards the fireplace and her body in the opposite direction, rolling over twice before coming to its final rest. He then recounted how he had sprung forward again and torn her pocket off. All the other details fell into place as, for once, King told the truth. Even the squashed candle he accidently trod on during his escape would later be found as he described and used to corroborate his account of the horrific events of that night. He also told PC Jones that he had asked Mrs Pullin to spend the night with him, whereupon she had said she would give him a knock on the head with a poker. He confessed again that he severed her head with his bean hook, adding 'twas not much of a blow', as if somehow this would provide some form of mitigation. He asked the police constables to write to his father explaining what he had done, as he could neither read nor write. King's confession to the two police officers whilst at Streatley, sealed his fate and would no doubt ensure a more rapid ride to a guilty verdict at the forthcoming trial.

The trial opened on Thursday, 27th February 1834, before Mr Justice Patterson. George King, aged 19, from Cumnor was charged with the 'wilful murder of Ann Pullin at Wantage on 30th August last'. In a steady voice, with no faltering, King pleaded 'Not guilty.' Right to the last, he was going for the outside chance that some idea might occur to rescue him from his fate, despite his having provided a full confession to the murder to two police constables the previous September.

The most poignant evidence at King's trial was given by Ann's stepson, James, now 13 years of age. Only six months ago, he had witnessed a scene that would live with him forever. He told the court, 'I and my sister went to bed about eight or nine o'clock. My mother used to go to bed about ten. On the next morning I got up between six and seven. When I went to bed the night before I left my mother alone. When I came downstairs I went to the front door and then went into the kitchen, saw my mother's head lying against the fireplace, and her body towards the door. There was a great deal of blood in the room. Went to the front door and met the milk boy coming up the steps. My mother kept her money in a dirtyish bag. She always kept a crooked sixpence, which she called her lucky sixpence.'

It would take more than a lucky sixpence to help George King as the evidence so patiently evaluated at the original inquest now poured forth in greater detail and without the hindrance of the emotional turmoil of that long weekend in Wantage at the end of August, 1833.

The bean hook was held aloft as a key exhibit as the details of the murder were related to the court by the prosecution. King glanced at it, but showed no emotion. There were no witness for the defence, and King declined to comment or attempt to defend himself. He was, as of right, provided with a legal defence team, a Mr Carrington and a Mr Stone.

Their task was hopeless, but with surprising guile, Mr Carrington cross-examined PC James Jones, trying to establish that his client had been threatened that, if he did not confess to the murder of Ann Pullin, 'a staple would be driven into the door (of the White Hart) and he would be chained to the dead body all night'. It was established that no one had heard such a threat or inducement to confess. A last, pathetic thrust by the defence lawyer was to say that throughout the trial no evidence had been provided to prove in strict legal terms that the deceased was in fact Mrs Ann Pullin of Wantage, so no case had been made out. This legal technicality was soon remedied by the coroner, Dr Cowcher.

King had come to the end of the road. His manner in court seemed to suggest that he had admitted to himself that there was no escape, no plan, no one else to blame, and he appeared to switch off in readiness for his inevitable fate. The newspapers described his 'sullen apathy and indifference' as he was sentenced to be executed on Monday, 3rd March at the county gaol.

He was empty, devoid of emotion, even when his mother visited him just before the sentence of the court was to be carried out. The *Reading Mercury* had spoken dramatically of the moment when 'the awful award of death will soon be meted out to the unfeeling monster'. The execution was not until midday, which would allow thousands of sightseers time to gather to witness King's death on the top of Reading gaol. It was a violent hanging. When the bolts were pulled just before midday, it was clear the fall was too short, and King suffered very slow strangulation as he thrashed and struggled for some minutes before he gave a last convulsive shudder and died. It was rumoured that the evil nature of his deed ensured the hangman would not oblige him with a clean hanging, and the public seemed to approve.

This horrific tale of murder has ended but there is still another twist that must be revealed. Is it significant? You must judge. When King was cut down after the customary hour left hanging, his head was shaved ready for burial and his description recorded for the files. Once his hair had been shaved clean off, there was on his skull a large fracture around three-quarters of an inch wide and five inches long. His mother revealed it was the result of falling from a hayloft some years previously. Did this have any bearing on his sudden irrational beheading of his kindly landlady? There was hardly any real monetary gain from his murderous deed and little chance of getting away with it in the long-term; so what was his motive: robbery, sexual rebuke, or a sudden irrational brainstorm?

At 2 pm, in the presence of the under sheriff for the county, he was unceremoniously placed in a hole in the prison grounds. The tragic tale of Ann Pullin was finally over, but the legacy of memories left to her children can only be imagined.

# WIZARD PALMER AND THE HAND OF GLORY

> 'Now open lock to the Dead Man's Knock!
> Fly bolt and bar, and band! —
> Nor move, nor swerve, joint, muscle or nerve,
> At the spell of the dead man's hand!
> Sleep all who sleep – Wake all who wake!
> But be as the Dead for the Dead Man's Sake.'
> Richard Harm Barham

Magic – and the claim to practise it – is one of the most enduring of all mysteries. Does magic exist? Are there real witches and wizards, or are we taken in by myth, legend, and scam? Enchantments, spells, potions, and talismen draw us into stories of the age-old battle between good and evil. Are they just tales, or do they contain some element of truth? It seems that such confrontations really do happen, and in certain Berkshire villages we can find the evidence.

This is the tale of the spell of the dead man's hand associated with the village of Winterbourne and a legendary Berkshire wizard of the first half of the 19th century known as Wizard Palmer of Boxford.

Our familiarity with fictional wizards, such as J.K. Rowling's boy wizard, Harry Potter, can blind us to the fact that wizards really did exist alongside the cult of witchcraft and witches, and many today claim such roles for themselves. Indeed, it wasn't until

1951 that British laws against witchcraft were fully lifted, and, as late as 1944, there was a trial at the Old Bailey under the original Witchcraft Act of 1735, in which Helen Duncan was convicted of being a witch, the last woman in England to be so.

Wizards of past times were also referred to as *cunning men*, and under that name they would give advice and guidance to those seeking remedies against misfortune and the unwanted attentions of the supernatural. The practice could involve both curing and cursing and was accepted by many village communities as traditional, rural folk magic, also called *cunning craft*.

As a practising Berkshire wizard, Palmer would be asked to exorcise or banish ghosts, and, as a cunning man, to supply the description of thieves who had stolen villagers' property. For a fairly hefty fee of around two shillings, the victim of a theft could obtain a consultation with Palmer in his small cottage by the River Lambourn, and by cunning means Palmer would write down the necessary description of the thief or thieves for the victim to trace. If the property had been lost rather than stolen, he could advise the owner where they might find it again.

By the late 1830s, Palmer had gained a reputation for solving Berkshire mysteries. For example, he was purported to have banished a shadowy, animal-like figure that haunted a derelict cottage by Wickham church and frightened the villagers. Legend has it he ordered heavy chains from Newbury, chained up the cottage, and contained the spirit within. By cunning, it is said he traced the person responsible for the mysterious severing of barge ropes along the Thames at Reading in 1841. He is also recorded as upsetting many people in Welford when he cast a spell to silence the church bells, as they got on his nerves, but he found himself evicted from his cottage by the squire for doing so.

However, Palmer is best remembered for his role in tackling the spell of the dead man's hand in the Berkshire village of Winterbourne. This tale involves a gruesome device of the black arts known as the *hand of glory*. Firstly we need to know how such a device as the hand of glory was actually created and all the magical powers it claimed to provide. This will help us understand Wizard Palmer's formidable task in dealing with its criminal use in Winterbourne.

Many claims to mysterious powers are associated with the

scaffold and its grim product: the dead body of a recently hanged or beheaded criminal. Such a body – or perhaps its fresh blood – was said to have mystical properties, and all over the world examples can be found that testify to this belief. In many counties in England, parents would attempt to take children onto the scaffold to have the hand of the corpse, damp with 'death sweat', rubbed against their skin as a cure for scrofulous diseases. Women would do the same in an attempt to remove their unsightly wens, cysts, or warts. Fresh blood from such a corpse was greatly prized in Germany, for example, where executioners in the 19th century made money by selling blood-sodden handkerchiefs, and in France a 'miracle' ointment was made from the fat of the executed. In many cultures, including the UK, keeping the fingers and thumbs of thieves as a talisman was believed to improve trade for a shopkeeper, or keeping a small bone in a purse was thought to stop it ever being empty. Even the rope that had choked the life from the criminal was claimed to have magical properties and would often be sold by the inch after an execution.

However, these 19th-century customs and many more besides, pale into insignificance when compared to the hand of glory as used in the county of Berkshire. For such a device, you needed to cut the hand from a freshly executed corpse, usually the right hand. More valued was a hand cut off during an eclipse of the moon, but this would be a rare commodity indeed. It then had to be wrapped in fabric taken from the corpse's shroud and squeezed hard to remove the blood. Once emptied, it was placed in an earthenware jar, with powered *zimort* ('cinnamon'), saltpetre, salt, and peppercorns, all powdered and dusted over the hand. After leaving it to marinate for 15 days, it had to be allowed to dry in the August sunshine or it could be put into an oven with vervain and fern. When it was grey, withered, and very dry, it was ready to be turned into the hand of glory.

To make it work for you, you needed some fat from another hanged man, as well as some of his hair, some *ponie* ('dung'), sesame, and virgin wax. From this you forged a candle with the hair as the wick. (The most wicked and abhorrent recorded cases of such candle-making used the finger of an unborn child cut from the mother's womb.) Using the hand as a candle-holder, with the candle wedged firmly between the grey, stiff fingers, you were now in a position to enter a house by candlelight that lit only your sight, while at the same time casting a spell over the inhabitants so that they remained in deep slumber if asleep, or motionless if awake, and totally blind to robbers. Some robbers preferred to wax the fingers and thumb of the hand itself and set these alight. If the thumb refused to light, it was a warning that someone was not asleep or had not yet fallen under its power. You would need to recite:

*Hand of Glory shining bright, lead us to our spot tonight.*
*Bind in sleep those now asleep. Bind awake those now awake.*

It was claimed also that the hand of glory was capable of defeating the cunning-art such as that possessed by Boxford's Wizard Palmer.

Cottage and farmhouse burglaries were a common occurrence across England as various rogues and vagabonds made their way from village to village, intent on stealing valuables in the dead of night. A series of such burglaries in the Winterbourne area led villagers to suspect the use of a hand of glory. No one had been able to hear, see, or realize they were being robbed, yet their valuables had disappeared by the dawn light, and they felt strangely groggy, as if suffering the effects of drinking heavy ale.

Wizard Palmer was consulted and he was able to offer some remedies to those wishing to protect themselves. It was recommended they smear their thresholds with ointments made from the blood of screech owls, or the fat of white hens. These were 'warning' ointments, said to counteract the spell that rendered one motionless, but the only sure way was to ambush the robbers and extinguish the flame of the hand of glory with a bucket of blue (which today we know simply as skimmed milk). This was the only substance capable of putting out its gruesome light and rendering it useless until a new candle was inserted.

But Palmer needed information about when a robbery using such a device of the black arts was to take place. His skills of cunning were supplemented by the less mysterious technique of employing informants to lurk about spying on others and listening to their conversations. This in itself was a risky business because, during the 1840s, lurking outside other people's houses and

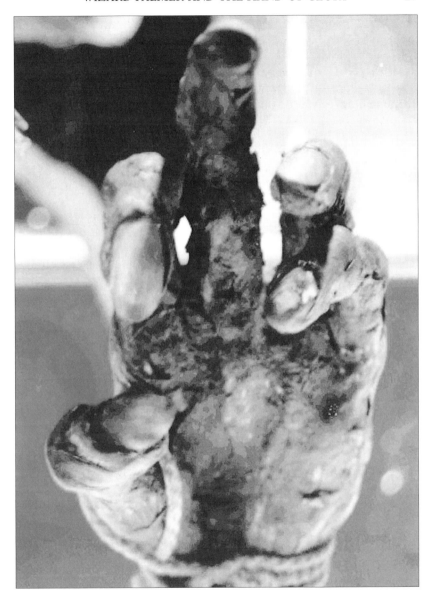

A dead man's hand, known as the hand of glory, was reputed to have magic properties.

cottages in order to overhear conversations by windows, walls and eaves was a criminal offence known as eavesdropping. So, just as the police had their informants, Palmer had his eavesdroppers, and information reached him about 'some family men who had been marking a crib in the wild, which they were about to prig with a glory'. Palmer's knowledge of this language used by criminals, known as flash or cant language, told him that thieves (*family men*) had been watching (*marking*) a house (*a crib*) in the village (*wild*) which they were about to rob (*prig*) with the hand of glory (*a glory*).

More work by his informants identified a farm just on the outskirts of Winterbourne, near Westbrook.

Palmer recruited a local village lad called Will Chamberlain, whom he judged could resist the power of the hand of glory long enough to defeat it. Some say he put a spell on the boy to make him immune, but this is not known for sure. Palmer and the boy hid in the farmhouse kitchen whilst the occupants feigned sleep. Palmer had not summoned the police but worked alone, as this enhanced his reputation as a wizard and cunning man. Perhaps he wanted the hand of glory for himself. Will secreted himself by the kitchen door, a bucket of blue by his side, whilst Palmer crouched further back to get a clear view of the approaching intruders and to judge the correct moment to break the spell of the dead man's hand.

As the night deepened, so the tale goes, they heard approaching footsteps and a soft glow appeared at the farmhouse door, which swung open to the chant,

*Hand of Glory shining bright, lead us to our spot tonight.*
*Bind in sleep those now asleep. Bind awake those now awake.*

At Palmer's precise command and just as the farmhouse threshold had been breached by two intruders, one of whom was holding the precious hand of glory in front of him, Will Chamberlain sprang forward and emptied the bucket of blue directly over the 'glory'. It fell to the floor, its thieving light extinguished, and the two robbers fled into the night. Palmer took charge of the 'glory', and, alongside his unrecorded fee from the farm owner, took away a much enhanced reputation as the Wizard of Boxford who rescued a village from total plunder.

He took away something else, of course. Its grisly origin we now well know, but what of its fate? In recent fiction, it certainly exists. When J.K. Rowling wrote about her wizard hero, Harry Potter, accidentally materializing in Borgin & Burkes, a shop specializing in the dark arts in dingy Knockturn Alley, he saw a long coil of hangman's rope, a staring glass eye, human bones, some evil-looking masks and rusty spiked instruments, and 'a withered hand on a cushion', a hand of glory, no less.

As I gaze at a real, grisly, withered and wrinkled, dirty grey hand of glory, preserved for all to see in Yorkshire's Whitby Museum, I wonder if this could possibly have seen criminal service in a certain Berkshire village and encountered a real wizard, Wizard Palmer.

No one knows what happened to Wizard Palmer; he disappeared some time in the 1850s, although not totally without trace. There is tale about an old wooden post at Welford that was known locally as Palmer's Post. Legend has it that he had driven out an evil spirit from a local farmer's son and nailed it to this post. Fanciful perhaps, but very soon after the M4 motorway was opened in the 1970s, stories began to surface about mishaps, silly accidents, cracks in a bridge, a police car and an ambulance suffering complete electrical circuit failures. It was only later that it was noticed that all these events had occurred around the original spot of Palmer's Post, long since felled and its foundations buried under motorway concrete.

Fact can be stranger than fiction and these events in the small Berkshire villages of Boxford, Wickham, Winterbourne, and Welford are certainly testimony to that.

# MURDER IN
# CLARENCE CLUMP

'I do not wish to cloud your brains by moving your hearts.'
George Russell, Defence Counsel,
*Regina v Gould*, 1862

All societies, all communities live with the act or, at least, the threat of murder occurring in their midst. Murder is a fact of life, but this does not make it any easier to accept or fully understand. Any understanding is more likely to occur when a background of conflict, violence, rivalry, or other confrontational behaviour is known and shown, but this does not make the deed right or acceptable. The act of murder is sometimes, however, beyond understanding and beyond belief, and this Berkshire tale is one such episode. It is a murder case of such an intensely emotional character that, even all these years later, it cannot but fail to anger and move the reader to wonder about the unpredictability of human behaviour and the depths to which it can sink.

It was 30th December, 1861, and life in the small, intimate community of Clarence Clump, off Clewer Lane, near Windsor, remained uneventful. Like all the cottages at this end of Clewer Lane, they were small, comfortable and respectable. It was one of those bright December days that starts to chill as the afternoon draws on and so is just a little too cold to be outside for long. Sarah Clark was busy with her needlework as her two children,

Clarence Clump was adjacent to Clewer Fields, though the original cottages have now been built over.

Harriet, aged 9, and her little brother, Daniel, aged 5, and two friends, Hannah Gould, aged 7, and Tommy Webb, aged 6, played in the house. Hannah Gould's mother had gone to work as a cleaner at Windsor Infirmary and Mrs Clark had said it would be no trouble to look after her.

All the children were playing well, but the time was approaching 1.30 in the afternoon and Hannah had to get back to start the fire so that the house was warm when her parents returned home. Her father, John Gould, was a bricklayer's labourer, but work was difficult to find this time of the year, so there was no telling what mood he might be in. She also needed to warm some potatoes over the fire for his dinner.

Hannah skipped out of Mrs Clark's cottage to her own home five doors down, followed by the whole gang of kids, who decided they might as well continue their games at Hannah's. There were no locked doors in this small community, so they all burst in, laughing and playing around. In the small parlour, they set about lighting the fire. Harriet, at 9, was in charge, and, as for most children of that age, lighting the parlour fire was a regular task. They all helped to coax it into life. Harriet and Hannah were the mothers getting the house ready, and Tommy and Daniel played at being their little children. About 3 pm, they heard the door open, and Hannah's father came in.

Harriet, who understood a little more about life, saw that he was, in her words, 'tipsy'. He was also very grumpy and, when he saw the other children in his parlour, shouted, 'You little Clarks, go out and shut the door after you.' He then turned to Hannah and said angrily, 'You are a very naughty little girl not to clean up the place.' Hannah quickly placed a large potato onto the fire, saying to her father, 'Father, I could not do it.'

Harriet was still there in the doorway, Tommy and Daniel quickly making their exit out of the front door. She looked knowingly at her friend Hannah and said, 'Hannah, will you come?' Before Hannah could answer, her father said sharply, 'No I want to do something to her.'

Just as Harriet was closing the door, she looked again at her friend sitting in the fireside chair, tears welling up in her eyes, her father reaching for something from a nearby shelf. Harriet shut the door and ran with her brother and Tommy Webb back to her house.

Sarah Clark was still engrossed in her needlework as the children returned. Harriet explained that Hannah's father had come home very tipsy and that Hannah had had to stay behind. It was around 3.30 pm when Sarah heard her name being called. It was Hannah's father, outside her cottage shouting, 'Mrs Clark, I want you.'

Sarah peered out and saw John Gould, agitated and looking, as she would say later, 'very wild as though his eyes were coming out of his head'.

Sarah had often seen Gould box Hannah's ears and strike her with his hand and she suspected he had beaten Hannah, so she went outside. John Gould turned and strode back to his house without another word. Sarah followed. Gould went inside, turned, and stood there, something in his hand. Sarah reached the door and saw blood everywhere and in Gould's hand a bloody, black-handled cut-throat razor. She screamed, not believing what she now saw.

Just inside the front door at the foot of the stairs was a terrible sight. It was Hannah Gould, crouched down on her knees, one hand supporting her head as she rested it on the bottom stair. Blood was pouring from her throat; her eyes tried to focus on Sarah. She was trying to speak, but could not. She seemed to be almost drowning in her own blood.

Sarah shouted to Gould, 'You vagabond, you have been and cut the child's throat.' Gould just stood there, clutching the bloody razor, repeating the phrase,

'I done it, I done it.'

Sarah Clark ran screaming from the house, crying, 'Murder, murder!' Several people came running towards her at her cries. Sarah turned back as if hoping the whole episode had been a dream, but to her horror it was much worse. Hannah was now lying outside the house, apparently flung into the street. Sarah screamed again and ran into her house, too distressed to do anything but protect her own children from an apparent mad man, with a razor.

At her cries of 'Murder', Samuel Wilkins, aged 12, who lived next door to Hannah, rushed out of his house, saw Mrs Clark running up the yard, and then saw his neighbour Mr Gould come out of his house holding Hannah. Gould then shouted, 'You little b–, I'll die for you,' and he flung his dying daughter against the wall opposite, about two yards away, so she was lying in the passage between her house and the next pair of cottages. He turned back into the house and Samuel ran across to Hannah and took her into his arms. She was alive but struggling for breath and Samuel could see clearly that her throat had been cut.

Charles Coker, a labourer, living three doors down was chatting with his friend George Beagley when they also heard Sarah's cries, and then the similar cries of others, so they dashed out to see what was happening. Charles saw young Samuel holding Hannah and John Gould standing in his door saying, 'I done it, I done it.' He could see the life blood pouring from Hannah. Coker and Beagley ran off to fetch a policeman. Coker returned with PC Peter Radbourne and pointed at John Gould, shouting, 'There he is.' Samuel had carefully laid Hannah down, and the police constable saw, in his words, a 'child lying struggling in the passage covered all over in blood'.

Samuel was in a terribly distressed state. He did not know what to do for the best as his friend Hannah fought for breath. He picked her up once more. Then Coker took the dying Hannah from young Samuel's arms and began to run with her a quarter of a mile to Windsor Infirmary.

PC Radbourne meanwhile said to Gould, 'You must consider yourself my prisoner and go with me to the police station.' Gould cried, 'No, I shall not,' and a struggle ensued. PC Radbourne managed to get on top of him to hold him down and George Beagley came to the constable's assistance. Also, a local plasterer, James Clark, arrived on the scene after hearing the commotion, and between them all they marched Gould off to the station in Windsor. As he walked with them, he repeated, 'I have done it.' He also said something else, which would become significant at the time of his trial. When Clark said to him, 'This is the last time you will walk up this street,' he said, 'I have done it because I am tired of my life.' As they got near to the police station, Gould said, 'I am happy now I have done it.'

Meanwhile, Coker had reached Windsor Infirmary, and staff sent for a surgeon named Ellison, who arrived just before 4 pm. There, lying on a small sofa in one of the rooms he saw a young child covered in blood. 'This child is quite dead,' he said. 'Its throat has been cut.' Coker was very distressed. He knew the child was alive as he ran as fast as he could to the hospital: she had opened her eyes, looking at him and struggling to speak, but it was too late. The concerned face of young Hannah's neighbour, Charles Coker, trying desperately to get her medical assistance, was the last person she would see. The surgeon discovered a five inch wound to her throat which had divided the jugular vein on the right side. She had died from loss of blood from the vein. He noted that she had been a very healthy girl, her life taken from her by the cruel slashing of a razor to the throat.

All of the witnesses and neighbours found the incident difficult to comprehend. This was not an attack by a stranger, not an attack in the course of a robbery, but a punishment from her own father, the ultimate punishment, death. From this moment on, the quest was to find a motive as to why a father would kill his only daughter, apparently for not keeping the house tidy. What devastation would Hannah's mother feel? She was working at the infirmary at the time her daughter was taken there. The *Windsor and Eton Express*, for 4th January, 1862 proclaimed, 'The crime is one of a most extraordinary character, owing to the entire absence of motive for its committal...There is no evidence even of those small provocations which children can sometimes give.'

Now would follow an inquest and trial to dissect how a small community like Clarence Clump could become a backdrop to such an horrendous crime. Was John Gould mad? Was he so intoxicated he became the murderer of his own daughter? What was this man really like?

Gould, born in Eton, had just turned 39 years of age and had lived in Windsor before moving to Clewer. He went to Porny's School in Eton and was originally apprenticed to a trunk-maker but proved unreliable and was not kept on. Then he worked as a general labourer, and, during the last five years in Clewer, he had been employed mainly as a bricklayers' labourer and had worked for nearly all the local builders, so that he was well known. He had a brother and a sister. He had married Anne; she already had a daughter, Elizabeth, aged 13, who lodged at the Three Elms, where she was a domestic servant. Hannah was the only child from the marriage and, as we now know, lived at home with her parents. Gould was known to be quite quarrelsome and he liked a drink, but this seemed an action beyond belief even for that kind of personality.

Hannah's horrific murder by her father took place on the Monday afternoon and the very next day, the last day of 1861, arrangements were made to take John Gould before the mayor, W.B. Holderness, for a hearing in the justice rooms in Windsor Town Hall. Concurrent with the hearing was to be Hannah's inquest in the council chamber; so witnesses could move directly from giving evidence in the judicial hearing to giving evidence before the coroner. The story all the witness told to the court was clear and without dispute as to what had happened. John Gould had cut his daughter Hannah's throat in their house, and then flung her out into the street in a violent and unbelievable act of cruelty. Perhaps if Gould had summoned medical help, leaving Hannah where she lay on the bottom stair, her life might have been saved. Why did he fling her into the street like a broken doll, hitting her against a wall?

No one could come to any understanding of this behaviour. Some witnesses to the hearing such as the police officer, Peter Radbourne, who arrested Gould, said, 'The prisoner appeared the worse for drink, but he was not drunk.' Harriet had called him 'tipsy', and others confirmed this. Superintendent Eager, who had joined PC Radbourne at the police station, told the hearing that Gould was 'excited from drink but not drunk'. Eager had said to Gould, 'What, in the name of God, did you do it for?' Gould said in reply, 'I came home to get some dinner, she commenced crying and very much annoyed me. I have done it and I am very sorry for it.'

The inquest before T.W. Marlin, sitting with a jury, heard the same tragic story as the witnesses moved from the justice rooms to the council chamber. It was clear from the inquest evidence that little Hannah was alive almost until the valliant Charles Coker reached the infirmary but death was said to have occurred during that nightmare journey as she was nestled in his arms. There was no question of doubt for the inquest jury, who returned a verdict of 'wilful murder' against John Gould.

The hearing before the mayor was adjourned until the next day, New Year's Day, Wednesday, 1st January, 1862. At the resumption of the hearing against John Gould, a new witness was called, who was able to add a fresh piece to the jigsaw. This witness had not been present at the scene of the crime. Rather, he was a long standing friend of John Gould, and what he had to say was astounding. His name was Reuben Turner, a carpenter, who lived in Clewer Lane, and around one or two o'clock on that fateful day, he went into the Prince of Wales pub, known locally as Rance's Beer House. There he saw his old school chum John Gould, who asked him to fetch in some more beer. They sat and drank together. Then, reported Reuben, Gould turned to him and said, 'I shall be locked up tomorrow.'

'Lord, Jack,' said Reuben, calling him by his nickname, 'don't talk like that. What are you going to be locked up for?'

'For murder,' replied Gould.

'Nonsense,' replied Reuben. 'Don't talk like that.'

Gould also told Reuben that he would not be alive on April 1st. After about twenty minutes of this depressing, drunken talk, Reuben left him in the tap room at the beer house.

This revelation stunned those present. This was even worse.

Although not naming his own daughter, he had said he intended to commit murder, which he did. He said he'd be locked up, which, of course, he was, and now all that remained was his own death by April 1st. So was this an elaborate and bizarre suicide plan? At the time of his arrest he said, 'I have done it because I am tired of my life.' He also said, 'I am happy now I have done it.' Was this the most selfish act a father could commit: murdering his own daughter for a triviality so he in turn could be executed by the state; taking an innocent young life as part of his own plan of death?

It was time for Gould himself to speak to the hearing. 'All as I have got to say is that it would not have happened if I had not been drinking. As soon as ever I gets anything to drink I don't know what I'm about. My head is all over covered in bruises and has been so knocked about and cut open, that makes me not know what I am about at times.'

The hearing was brought to a close by the mayor, who committed Gould for trial at the next assize at Reading. The charge was 'the wilful murder of Hannah Gould'. He was escorted by Police Sergeant Noble through the booing hissing crowds, some of whom lashed out at him, and on to Windsor station, where he was taken in a closed compartment to Reading. Once on the train, Gould turned to Noble and said, 'I'm glad to get off from that mob.' As the train approached Reading, he could see the gaol to the side of the track and remarked to Noble, 'This is going to be my last home in this world.'

It was clear from the media coverage that Gould was regarded as either wicked or totally insane, or perhaps both. No one could excuse this as drunken behaviour. It seemed the forthcoming trial would certainly yield a guilty verdict, but the jigsaw was not yet complete.

Reading had just built new assize courts adjoining the ancient Abbey gateway in the area called Forbury, and Gould's case was its first murder trial in these new surroundings. The judge was Baron Channell from the Oxford circuit, and the trial was scheduled for an early start on Friday, 28th February, 1862. By the time the court opened at 9 am, the crowds were enormous, and the galleries soon filled to capacity. The local paper reported, 'The galleries and the other spaces appropriate to the spectators were soon crowded by persons of genteel appearance and among them was a considerable sprinkle of females.'

There was an audible gasp as John Gould was escorted into the dock. He entered a guilty plea to the charge of 'having on 30th December last, wilfully murdered his daughter, Hannah Gould, aged seven years in Clewer Lane, Windsor'.

Gould had not instructed any counsel to defend him, but, for the prosecution to succeed, it was essential that due process of law was followed and this meant the defendant had to have a defence lawyer. Mr Blaney, the undersheriff, had instructed George Russell to defend the prisoner. This would be difficult, given the procession of prosecution eye-witnesses to be called, plus the fact that there were no witnesses that could be called in Gould's defence. Russell, however, had a plan of defence that was skilfully and artfully woven and caused many ripples far beyond the court room. J.O. Griffits for the prosecution, began his case by reminding the jury that 'the prisoner, John Gould, stands charged with the most serious crime known to the laws of this country'.

It is not difficult to imagine the gasps and sounds of incredulity that escaped the enthralled spectators as witness after witness told the terrible story of the murder of Hannah Gould. Her pathetic little blood-soaked body thrown to the ground by her callous, murdering father. Russell, however, was careful in his questioning of each eye-witness, not to discredit their account. These he accepted. What he was more concerned about was whether John Gould had been acting oddly over that week or the weeks leading up to the murder. Some witnesses agreed he had been 'odd' all week. Others were less sure that he was any different.

Without any witnesses for the defence, Russell was building together some tenuous comments from the prosecution witnesses, hoping that some extenuating circumstances at least might be revealed. Did the witnesses know about his earlier suicide attempts some years back? Did they know he had suffered injuries to the head in a brawl with the police years ago that left him with a dangerous head wound?

Some older friends such as Reuben Turner were aware of these occurrences; others were not, or chose to forget. George Beagley, who had known Gould for five or six years, would only concede he had been looking 'sullen' of late. In fact, George revealed to the court that he saw John Gould heading home from the pub to his house and shouted out to him, 'Halloo, John, no trade today?' Gould did not reply but just 'looked sullen'. Had he seen a man intent on murder, or a man temporarily insane?

It was this angle that was pursued by Russell. He wanted the jury to consider Gould's state of mind at the time he committed the act. In order to get the jury to understand what this meant, he asked the judge's permission to read the definition of murder as it stood at that time. He was a most eloquent speaker and he addressed the jury thus,

'What is murder? It is thus defined by Lord Coke, *"It must be committed by a person of sound memory and discretion who unlawfully killeth any reasonable creature in being and under the King's peace – with malice aforethought, either expressed or implied."* Does the evidence that has been laid before you today justify you in saying that this man committed an act which comes within this definition?'

He narrowed it down and asked the jury quite directly whether John Gould was 'of sound memory and discretion *at the time he committed the act*'? Both prosecution and defence had dismissed any notion that drunkenness could be seen as an excuse. But how about insanity? That was an excuse.

Russell went on to draw a picture of Mrs Gould sitting alone in her little cottage awaiting their verdict upon her husband and unable by law to come to his defence. We do not know, of course, whether she would have spoken on his behalf had the law permitted, but he left it in the air, hinting that she possibly held the key to his behaviour that day. In other words she may have been able to say he was suicidal; that he was acting irrationally; that he was possibly insane.

We will never know. Telling the jury he did not want to 'cloud their brains by moving their hearts', he was left with one final plea. 'Now, when my voice has ceased to ring in your ears and my tongue is still, I hope that a far more powerful voice – I hope that God's "still small voice" – will speak to you, and enable you to pronounce as the verdict, leaping as it were from your hearts, "not guilty". As my last word, I demand that which is your duty to do: justice, justice, justice; and demand that which is your prerogative: mercy, mercy, mercy.'

In his summing up, Baron Channell reminded the jury that it was a prima facie case of murder and that no witnesses had been called on behalf of the prisoner. I suspect that as a result of Mr Russell's quite remarkable closing speech for the defence, the judge expected the jury to take its time debating the issues. Having sent them out to consider the verdict, he then took on a robbery case in the same court room. However, only ten minutes passed before the jury reached a unanimous verdict, but they then had to wait for an hour until the robbery case had been heard.

The tension was electric when the jury finally filed in and the foreman pronounced the verdict: 'Guilty'.

The gasps became cries, and someone sobbed. Baron Channell placed the black cap upon his head and, addressing the prisoner, said: '. . . that you be taken from hence to the place from whence you came and from thence to the place of execution, and that you be there hanged by the neck until you are dead and that your body be afterwards buried within the precincts of the gaol in which you may now be confined. And may the Lord have mercy upon your soul.'

It was silent. Gould was detached and showed no emotion. A few sobs from the gallery broke through. It was over. Gould was escorted to the cells, and the public flocked out.

It was Friday, 14th March, 1862. The scaffold had been skilfully erected above the entrance to Reading gaol. It was high enough for the thousands of expected spectators to see Gould's death by hanging. Even so, the authorities were worried about injuries from the crush, as the approach to Forbury narrowed as you got closer, and so they opened up meadows adjoining the prison for the overflow of visitors. Well over 4,000 people began to gather. Vendors of oranges, nuts, and watery lemonade were making their own killing, 'whilst others of a suspicious appearance were to be observed cautiously moving about, apparently intent upon anything but honesty', so reported the local paper's news correspondent.

What had also been the subject of much media coverage since the trial and right up to the day of execution was the attempt by a whole range of influential people to persuade the Home Secretary for mercy and a stay of execution. George Russell's stirring defence had moved many hearts and, some would say, definitely clouded their brains as they sought an audience with Sir George Grey, the Home Secretary. This included the Mayor of Reading himself, who, with other influential Berkshire inhabitants, made his way to London on the eve of the execution, seeking mercy for a man whose crime, they claimed, fell outside the true definition of murder.

The law was to take its course, said Grey, as the deputation now found itself still in London on the day of execution. Would there be a last minute stay of execution? This thought added an extra tension to Friday morning as noon, the declared execution time, approached, and many false claims of a respite circulated. Would he or wouldn't he be hanged? Rumours and gossip were as rife as the pickpockets in the crowd.

What of Gould himself? Gould had found God and had been absorbed in religious readings since his incarceration. His stepdaughter, Elizabeth, in a very moving visit to the gaol, had given him a Bible and urged him to read it. This he did, and was now taken over by it. He wrote letters to his wife and stepdaughter, his brother and sister, asking for forgiveness and saying that they should not be concerned about his punishment, which was a just one. So, unlike the group calling themselves 'the memorialists', who were campaigning on his behalf, Gould was not seeking earthly mercy, only that from his Maker. He also wrote a great deal about 'that cursed drink' and preached abstinence to any in the prison who would listen.

The gaol clock struck noon; as it did so, the prison governor, Mr Ferry, together with the undersheriff, Mr Blandy, entered Gould's cell, where he was on his knees praying. It seems that Gould had made a considerable impression on the prison staff. Rather than shun a man who murdered his own daughter in cold blood for a triviality, all the officers of the gaol stood in a line outside his cell, and, as Gould passed, he shook their hand and said in a clear voice, 'I hope I shall meet you in Heaven.' Calcraft, the executioner, was the final man to greet him, but not with a handshake. He set about pinioning him in preparation for the 'drop into eternity'. The sound of the waiting crowd grew louder as the procession of death crossed the prison yard, led by the governor and the undersheriff, and with Calcraft supporting Gould, still clutching the Bible given to him by his stepdaughter.

They climbed the steps to the scaffold above the prison gates, high above the teeming masses below. The noise was deafening – boos, cheers, clapping, shouting, laughter – every sound merging into a backdrop of continuous noise until Calcraft placed the noose around the condemned man's neck.

Gould turned to catch the eye of the prison chaplain, who crossed over to him. He whispered he would like the Bible returned to his stepdaughter, with his love; the chaplain took it from him and stood back in line. Gould's last words were, 'Give my love to my people and tell them I remember them.'

Calcraft drew the bolt; the trapdoor opened with a thud; and Gould fell, jerking back as the end of the rope took his full body weight. He shook violently with two or three convulsions as the life was forced out of him, and he was dead. The crowd cheered and shouted. For many, it was pure entertainment as well as seeing justice carried out for a child murderer. The body was left to hang for the statutory one hour before being cut down and buried. The crowds began to drift away.

When Gould first approached Reading gaol, he saw it from the train, remarking how it would be his last home on Earth. As he hung, there, it was realized by the undersheriff, that Gould dangling from the scaffold would be visible from trains coming into Reading, not a sight every passenger would welcome. He arranged for a cloth screen to drop down, concealing the view. He was not to know it, but this spectacle was the last public execution in the town of Reading.

The prediction Gould made that terrible Monday afternoon in Rance's beer house to his old school friend Reuben Turner had certainly come true. He was dead by April 1st, with eighteen days to spare.

# THE MYSTERY OF THE
# THATCHAM COFFIN

*'Our birth is nothing but our death begun, as the tapers
waste the moment they take fire.'*

Edward Young

The pleasant Berkshire town of Thatcham boasts a splendid
Norman church, which over the years has seen additions and
changes that pay tribute to the many local initiatives that have
kept its fabric in reasonable order. Like most parish churches
around the country, the battle to restore and update is a
continuous one.

And so it was on the evening of Tuesday, 12th February, 1929,
that a public meeting was held in Thatcham Parish Hall to
consider the seriously deteriorating state of the bells and belfry of
the church. For many this was a particularly passionate debate, as
it involved not merely reconstructing and strengthening a rotting
belfry but possibly replacing the bells altogether. Church bells are
part of the very soul of a church, its special local 'voice', and the
suggestion to replace the six existing bells with eight new ones
brought the debate to new heights.

Some wanted more consideration given to the repair of the
existing bells, whilst others felt it was best to rip everything out
and start again. So began the journey that takes us to that
mysterious and intriguing pinnacle of any church: the belfry. This

particular belfry was soon to yield up a macabre secret and leave us with an unsolved mystery to this day.

Parishioners worked hard throughout the following months to raise the money for repairs estimated at anywhere from £344 to £500, depending on what was decided about the bells. By the summer, they had already raised over £200 and were on target to start renovation work by the autumn. By November, most of the money was in place and work had begun on the final plan to repair the existing bells and add a new one, replace their oak frames with iron, and rebuild the rotting belfry floor area.

Work was progressing well but one particular workman, Cecil Joseph Maskell, was soon to discover that the belfry was hiding a grim secret. For Cecil, a local carpenter and joiner, this was his first day on the job and it would leave him with a story to tell well into his old age. It was Monday, 25th November, around 2 pm, when Cecil and his working companion, Joseph William Sidney Adnams, a bricklayer, were high up in the ringing chamber pulling down the ceiling which was the floor to the belfry itself. They were wading through a mass of rubble and old sawdust, swiftly ducking as lumps of ceiling board fell and enveloped them in dust and débris. Cecil and Joseph then took their shovels to clear away the mess for later disposal. Cecil shovelled up what he thought was an old bell-rope guide that had fallen from the belfry floor above, but he was very much mistaken. It was a tiny coffin: a perfectly formed, but very small, elm coffin. This, in itself, was a mystery, because workmen had been into the belfry above earlier in the week and so should have seen this on the floor, between the joists, had it been there. It seems that it had been dislodged from a hiding place somewhere close to the clock tower itself. Maybe it was the vibration of demolition that had sent it tumbling to the feet of the workmen below.

Perhaps it was its time to be found.

Cecil and Joseph gazed at it, not knowing what to think. Then they decided to open it. The coffin lid was fastened by four small nails, which soon gave way to Cecil's gentle prising, and the lid was removed. What they saw shocked them both. Inside were the mummified remains of a baby. It had been wrapped in some kind of patterned shroud, now barely discernible, and was resting on the remains of a brown paper bag.

The two working companions wasted no time in descending the thirty-three steps to the tower entrance to seek out the vicar of Thatcham, the Revd Reginald Charles Moore, and tell of their discovery. Shown the coffin with its mummified remains, he in turn informed the police. Sergeant Simmonds inspected the gruesome find, wrapped it carefully in a motor rug and drove it in the police car to be safeguarded in the parish room awaiting arrangements to set up an inquest. Meanwhile, a Thatcham doctor, James Robert Beagley, was shown the body by the police and confirmed it was that of a newborn infant, parts of which were in a good state of mummification. It was now impossible to determine its sex, but he judged that death had occurred around twelve to fifteen years earlier.

More sinister, however, was the discovery by the police sergeant and the examining doctor of a piece of stout string, around a foot long, a frayed part of which was by the baby's neck. Was this a murder?

Why would a murdered baby be given such an elaborate coffin? And why would it be secreted in a church belfry? This was just the beginning of a whole range of questions posed by this bizarre discovery. The remains were then taken to the church sacristy to wait for the inquest in the parish room, under the guidance of the coroner, Mr S.V. Pinniger

At the opening of the inquest on the morning of Saturday, 30th November, 1929, it was decided by the coroner that the usual practice of inquest juries not viewing the body was inappropriate, and he required all eight members to inspect the grisly remains, hoping it would assist them to ask their own, perhaps more pertinent, questions and perhaps also build up a picture of exactly what had occurred and why. Who was the baby in the hidden elm coffin and how and when did the child die?

The news of the discovery soon spread around Thatcham, the questions on most people's lips being 'How did it get there?' and 'Who was responsible?' If they had hoped for an early answer, they were going to be disappointed. Such a mysterious discovery required more time to investigate, especially if murder was involved, and so the inquest was adjourned for two months for police and other inquiries to be made. Before the Saturday adjournment, however, it was clear that the feeling at the inquest was that the circumstances were suspicious. The *Newbury Weekly News,* reporting on the proceedings, announced, 'The evidence revealed one factor which could not be regarded as anything but a sinister aspect – within the wrappings round the body was a stout piece of string, part of which had rotted. From its position in relation to the body, and other circumstances, Dr Beagley gave it as his opinion that the most popular conclusion to arrive at was that death occurred from strangulation.'

So, this chance discovery by Cecil was beginning to look more and more like a murder inquiry. The murder of an innocent, newborn baby. But, there was another complication to this mystery that needed to be considered. As the jury and the witnesses examined the mummified remains laid out on the table before them, were they seeing a human being which had lived outside the womb and was then murdered, or had the baby never experienced an independent existence? Dr Beagley had already given the probable cause of death as strangulation but the coroner then asked the doctor a very simple but crucial question: 'Had it ever been alive outside the womb?'

The doctor had to admit that he could not tell. He could ascertain that it was a full-term child, to within about one month, but it was now impossible to tell if it had actually had an independent existence. So, although the presence and position of the stout cord would indicate foul play, it would have to be established that the child had been born prior to strangulation for a murder to have been committed. It was possible that the child was stillborn. But why murder a stillborn baby? Whoever was responsible for this act may have not realized the baby was already dead, or may have wished to make sure that it was dead. It had already been confirmed by Dr Beagley that no other form of injury could be seen on the skull or remaining bones. No other marks of violence, such as depressed cracks showing as fractures, could be seen whatsoever.

So, had the baby been murdered or had it died by other means, an accident perhaps? All theories had to be considered. But then we come to the issue of the tiny body's location and concealment: what is to be made of this?

The foreman of the jury asked, 'How did the coffin get into the tower?' Speculation then ensued as to whether this was part of an

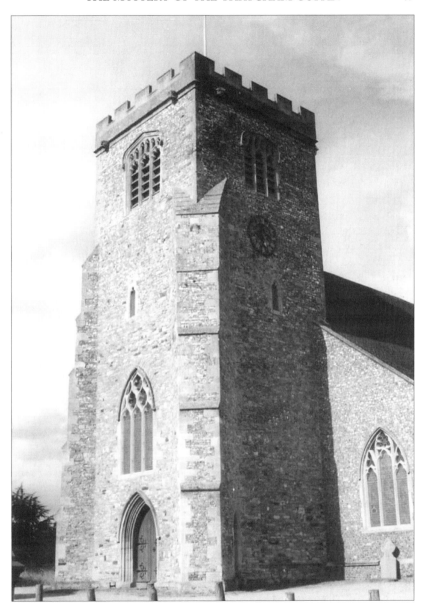

The parish church tower in Thatcham, where the tiny elm coffin was discovered.

old ritual of that time for stillborn babies. Cecil and Joseph had already given evidence that in their view it was a deliberate act of concealment. From the angle of its fall to their position in the ringing chamber, it would have been on the south side of the tower, almost immediately under the church clock. They felt that workmen who had already been in the belfry area over the previous week would have seen it, if it had not been hidden. Joseph said that he had been working there on at least three previous occasions and was sure he would have seen such an object if it had been left on the belfry floor. It seemed it had been tucked away on a ledge high up. It was now a police matter to determine whether a crime had been committed and if there had been a deliberate act of concealment.

Perhaps the mother of the child would come forward now the discovery had been made public. Possibly the baby was illegitimate. Attitudes were still very blinkered in the early 20th century, when it was likely to have been born. But, the mother had taken the pregnancy to full term, so had she been kept hidden herself until her baby was born, strangled, and concealed in the church? Was there someone who conspired with her?

The questions kept coming as the mummified remains were carefully returned to the coffin and kept securely in the church sacristy in readiness for the recommencement of the inquest on 1st February, 1930. The vicar had already decided that he regarded the child as having had a separate existence from its mother and would, when permitted, arrange for a Christian burial.

And what about the coffin itself? It was made of elm and expertly shaped. It was hardly indicative of the hasty arrangements of a murderer. Inside the coffin lid were four strange marks that no one could decipher. Would these give a clue as to the occupant? Was it part of a ritual after all? The mystery of the Thatcham coffin deepened.

The inquiry was a complex one. It was more a task for a historian than for the police, but it was important to try to ascertain who would have had access to the belfry around the time of the coffin's secretion, and why such a macabre act had been perpetrated. It had already been established how easy it was to carry the baby's coffin tucked under one arm whilst climbing the steps to the ringing chamber; the only tricky bit was climbing the ladder up to the belfry itself. Perhaps the coffin's secretion was carried out by flickering candlelight in the dead of night.

Some with more down-to-earth theories suggested that it had merely been forgotten. But why the cord, and why place the coffin in the belfry? Again, more questions than answers, but that's the nature of most real mysteries. The *Newbury Weekly News* had this to say about it being merely a lapse of memory: 'There is the possibility that it may have been the intention of the person or persons who concealed it to secrete it temporarily; if so, why was it not removed later? One cannot imagine its existence being totally forgotten.'

The two months set aside to make inquiries in preparation for the resumption of the inquest did yield some new information but also raised even more questions. The same jury, under the guidance of the same coroner, resumed its duties.

A new witness, found as a result of police investigations into the origin of the coffin, was a craftsman coffin maker and local undertaker, Thomas Maccabee. After 64 years' experience, man and boy, there was little he did not know about the business, and he was able to throw a new spanner in the works. He dated the timber of the coffin to around 45 or 50 years old. This did not mean, of course, it had been in the belfry that long, or had indeed been made into a coffin all those years ago, but it was possible. Also, he did concede that as an apprentice he himself might even have made the tiny coffin during his early training, as he had made many like it.

Police Sergeant Simmonds had obtained other expert information about the coffin lid and discovered it was English elm and at least 20 years old. The marks on the inside of the lid were those of the timber merchant, which told the expert that it had been cut from a 25 ft board. So, at least the mystery of the markings on the inside of the coffin lid was now solved. Other information concerned the stout cord, which was likely to have been used as a ferret line, and the brown paper bag lying under the body in the coffin was of a similar type to those made by home workers in Thatcham many years before.

Mr Maccabee confirmed that it was past practice to make a deal with the sexton to bury stillborn babies at the same time as a regular burial. In evidence to the inquest he said, 'Years ago, when there was a stillborn child, it was the rule to take it to the sexton with two shillings for its burial, and it used to be kept for some time until the burial of an ordinary person, so that it could be buried in the same grave.' Such a baby might be kept for up to three or four months before being buried. However, putting the coffin into the belfry, meanwhile, was not something he had ever heard of before.

The vicar, the Revd Moore, had been busy during the previous two months trying to locate some clues in the parish registers, but, of course, these would not normally include any information other than straightforward baptisms and burials; the mystery baby was hardly likely to be identified through this route. But the Revd Moore did offer a possibility that it was a male child baptized on 19th June, 1884. The vicar had stumbled across the concept of baptisms *in extremis*. This was the practice of an emergency baptism by a layman. Perhaps the baby was stillborn or dying, and, if the priest were unable to arrive in time, the midwife or any other volunteer could, in front of witnesses, baptize the dead or dying child. Why had the vicar plumped for that particular date? The entry for 19th June, 1884 stood out because there were no follow-up records: no death entry and no burial entry, yet this male child had been recorded as being baptized *in extremis* at this time. What happened to him? Was he the baby in the belfry?

It is significant that the last time restoration work had been carried out in the belfry was in 1882. In fact, it was done by Mr Maccabee's father, who had repaired the belfry floor; so it was likely that someone would have spotted the coffin at that time, had it been there. This suggests, therefore, that the coffin had been hidden after 1882, thus supporting the vicar's theory.

However, we are no closer to the motive for the coffin's secretion, even if the vicar's enlightening research has pinpointed the time it occurred and the sex of the child. The emergency baptism discovered by the vicar does not necessarily mean that the baby concerned did die; he may have recovered after all and so did not appear as a death entry in the register.

It seemed there was nowhere left to go except to close the inquest with an open verdict, the coroner concluding, 'From the condition of the remains, it is not possible to find the cause of death. Probably strangulation with the string found by the side of the body.'

However, he wished to ensure that the remains now received the burial denied to them all those years ago. He also wanted to keep the possibility of solving the mystery of the Thatcham coffin alive; so he asked for the child's remains to be placed in a new coffin, in case there were yet clues to be found from that baby's original resting place. Mr Maccabee was commissioned to make a coffin for the baby. Perhaps for the second time, it would lie in one of his creation, but this time in the consecrated ground of the parish church.

On Thursday, 6th February, 1930, Thatcham's mystery baby was finally laid to rest.

# THE HEYWOOD PARK TRAGEDY

'*The only thing that ever came back*
*from the grave that we know of was a lie.*'
Marilla Ricker (1840-1920)

Ronnie's Auntie Fleet was worried. Something was seriously wrong. Her nephew Ronnie, aged 12, came to stay with her on Saturday at her house in East Burnham, and, as arranged, he had set off back home on the Sunday evening by bus. Home was a pleasant semi-detached house, 8 Heywood Avenue in White Waltham, where he lived with his mother, baby sister, Connie, just 16 months old, and Ernest, his mother's boyfriend, whom he knew as 'Daddy'.

It was a lovely, early autumn evening on Sunday, 11th September, 1932. Ronnie reached home around 9 pm. Ernest opened the door and to Ronnie's first question, 'Where's Mum?', he told Ronnie she had gone up to Birmingham and he was looking after baby Connie and him till she got back. Ronnie cried. He was really looking forward to seeing his mother and did not understand why she had gone away. Ernest showed Ronnie a note his mother had written which said, 'Dear Ronnie, I have gone to Birmingham so be a good boy, Daddy and Connie will look after you, love Mum.'

Ernest said that he should really go back to stay with his auntie, but it was too late to go that night. Connie was asleep in her cot.

Ronnie was upset and puzzled. Ernest told him to buck up and Mum would be back soon, and he made them both some supper. Ronnie was still upset, so Ernest said he could sleep in the big bed with him and that's what happened.

On the Monday morning, Ernest got up, made the tea, and called Ronnie, who came downstairs with his baby sister in his arms. They all had breakfast together, Ernest explaining that it was best both Ronnie and Connie went to stay with Auntie Fleet at Burnham until their mother returned. He packed them a change of clothes and took them as far as the trading estate, where he put them on a bus, telling the conductor to put them off at Farnham Common. When Miss Mabel Fleet answered her door that late Monday morning, lo and behold, nephew Ronald was back, now accompanied by her niece Constance.

At first she was surprised, but, when Ronnie gave her a note from his 'dad', she was puzzled and then worried. The note read, 'Miss Fleet, I have sent Connie down to you because she will be looked after better down there than I can until her mum gets back. She is my baby as you know.' Ronnie wasn't mentioned as he could speak for himself. He explained, with a tear in his eye, that his mother had left him a note about going to Birmingham and he didn't know why, or when she would come back.

Mabel Fleet could not understand why Ronnie and Connie's mother, her sister Gwendoline, had not told her about such a trip. Mabel had never met Ernest, who had been living with Gwen at Heywood Park as her husband for the last two months, so she did not have any particular opinion of him. She did know, though, that he used to be a baker but that he wasn't in work at present.

Gwen had met Ernest Hutchinson a few years before, on 5th July, 1930, when he became a lodger at Gwen's old home, 4 Court View in Maidenhead, where she lived with her husband, Thomas William Warren. Gwen was already a single mother when she became Mrs Warren in 1924. Her daughter Marjorie was born in 1916, and then came Ronald, born in 1920. When Ernest Hutchinson moved in with the Warrens to supplement the family income as the lodger, he wasted no time in flirting with Gwendoline, and, the day after he moved in, he and Gwen ran off with her children to start a new life. Thomas was devastated.

Her affair with Ernest Hutchinson lasted seven or eight weeks and then Gwen wrote to Thomas for his forgiveness and asked if she could come back and start again. Thomas agreed. She was pregnant with Hutchinson's child, and baby Constance Rosina was born in April 1931. Just over a year later, on 10th July, 1932, Gwen took the children and left Thomas for good. She moved into the rented semi-detached house at 8 Heywood Avenue with Ernest Hutchinson, and here Ronnie now lived with his baby sister, Connie, his 16-year-old sister Majorie having left home to make her own way in the world.

Mabel Fleet took her niece and nephew into her cosy East Burnham home and looked after them, worried about what exactly was going on in her sister's life. She was used to Gwen's ways and sudden impulses, but this was out of character. Whilst Gwen had always been the flirtatious and adventurous one, Mabel had taken on the role of the sensible, reliable sister. She had never married and was the highly respected headmistress of East Burnham School. She loved her sister but her morally dubious behaviour did concern her.

By Wednesday, 14th September, Mabel was very worried indeed about events and then a postcard arrived from Gwen, with the briefest of messages. It said, 'Staying till Friday. Will write to you so please keep Connie and Ronnie till then,' and it was signed 'Gwen'. This was reassuring in some senses, but Mabel's worries turned to unease. It did not feel right, so she decided to look after Connie and send Ronnie back home to find out more from Ernest.

Ronnie got the bus and arrived back at Heywood Avenue just after midday that Wednesday. He met Ernest just as he was setting off from the house carrying an attaché case. He explained to Ronnie that he was off to Birmingham to meet up with his mother and they would both come back together. In the meanwhile, Ronnie was to go back to his auntie's house. He gave him a note for Miss Fleet, took him to Maidenhead railway station, and left him to make his way to East Burnham, whilst Ernest took a London-bound train en route to Birmingham.

You can imagine Mabel Fleet's shock at Ronnie appearing once more on her doorstep clutching a note. It read, 'Dear Miss Fleet, Just a few lines to you saying I am going to Birmingham to Gwen for a few days, so no use writing her until Friday. Keep Ronnie and Connie until then.' That was it. Mabel Fleet needed to take action.

She decided that she and Ronnie would travel back to Heywood Park together that very evening. Perhaps there had been a row of some kind, and, just as Gwen had left Thomas, maybe she had left Ernest. But why go to Birmingham? Mabel organized a neighbour to care for Connie whilst she and Ronnie set off for number 8 Heywood Avenue. For Miss Mabel Fleet and her nephew, Martin Ronald Warren, this day, 14th September, 1932, would change their lives forever, and somehow Auntie Fleet was already sensing this.

It was around 6.30 pm when they reached the snug semi-detached in Heywood Avenue, the front gate welcoming them to 'Davyholme'. The house was eerily silent. She called through the letterbox and got Ronnie to peer through, but he could see nothing and the house appeared empty. What on earth had happened? Miss Fleet was very worried but did not want to alarm Ronnie unduly. They had to break in. Scouting round the outside, they found a slightly open larder window, just big enough for Ronnie to climb through. Once inside, Ronnie opened the back door and let in his auntie.

There was no sign of Gwendoline at all, and Ernest certainly had not changed his mind and returned. Miss Fleet wondered what was going on as she explored the house with Ronnie. Something was very wrong, and suddenly Mabel realized what it was. The house was too empty. Where was the piano? A sofa was missing, and an oak table had gone. She felt a chill of confusion and apprehension. In Ronnie's bedroom, the bed was missing, and the bedclothes were lying untidily on the floor. Ronnie started crying. The house looked abandoned, his own room was not the bedroom he had left last Saturday. Gwen and Ernest's room looked almost tidy, but some clothes were strewn on the floor and the double bed was unmade. That was enough for Mabel, she decided to go to the police and ushered Ronnie out of the house.

Miss Fleet then recalled that the next-door neighbour was an ex-Reading Borough police officer, so she went to seek his assistance. The neighbour, Joseph Thomas Hutton, immediately agreed to go back to the house to have a look round for some clues as to what had happened.

It was just as Miss Fleet had described: no one was about. Joseph said he had not seen her sister for three or four days. He last spoke to Ernest about three days ago when he had asked after

Gwendoline and was told that she was in bed and would probably make a day of it.

Hutton went upstairs to look at the bedrooms; the doors were open except to the front spare bedroom, which Miss Fleet had not entered. He knocked and called but there was no answer. He opened the door. It was empty except for a quantity of bedding rather precariously piled up in the corner on top of a single bedstead, as if awaiting the removal men. It did not seem right to have been left like this, so he went into the room to investigate further. On top of this pile were rolled-up bedclothes and underneath was a spring mattress that was balanced on the metal structure of the top half of a single bed. This, in turn, was lying on an overlay and last of all, at the bottom, was a quilt. Cautiously feeling under the rather bulky quilt, he froze as he felt the cold, stiffened limbs and skin of a body.

He quickly pulled off the bedding, spring mattress, and metal bed frame that had been used to weigh down the quilt over the chest and face of the corpse, to reveal the body of Gwendoline Annie Warren, his 37-year-old neighbour. She was fully dressed but not wearing any shoes. Even his experience of working in the police had not prepared him for this terrible sight. He covered her with the quilt and shot downstairs to prevent Miss Fleet and Ronnie being confronted with the horror of seeing Gwendoline lying stone cold dead in the spare room. He ushered them out of the house and telephoned the police.

This had all the signs of a brutal murder; so, as well as the local police, the Chief Constable of Berkshire, the Hon. Humphrey Legge, was called, and soon 8 Heywood Avenue was sealed off as a crime scene. The body was then removed by ambulance to Maidenhead mortuary ready for a post-mortem.

The police surgeon, Dr Wilson, could not be sure as to the exact cause of Mrs Warren's death, and sought permission from the coroner to send certain body parts to the forensic laboratories at the Home Office for expert analysis. Permission was granted and later that evening, Inspector Barrett and Sergeant Burbridge were on their way to London with their gruesome package. Meanwhile, the hunt was on for Ernest Hutchinson and the following description of him was issued: 'A man aged 41, 5ft 7ins to 5ft 10ins tall, fresh complexion, brown or ginger hair, grey eyes, wearing a grey suit and heavy black boots, no hat or coat and carrying an attaché case.'

Some 24 hours after the tragic discovery of Gwendoline Warren's body, a report was received from Southend police, who had apprehended one Ernest Hutchinson in a boarding house in Broadway Market, close to Southend railway station. He was with a women called Doris Dew and they had booked in the previous evening as man and wife. So, far from being in Birmingham, as he had claimed to Mabel and Ronnie, he had fled to the East Coast with another woman.

So begins the mystery of how Gwendoline Annie Warren actually died – was it indeed murder or rather some bizarre accident, and, if murder, who was the murderer?

As Inspector Barrett and Sergeant Burbridge from Maidenhead police were still in London waiting for the analysis of the body parts they had delivered, they set off to Southend to bring in Hutchinson for questioning. Meanwhile, the Southend police informed Hutchinson that the Maidenhead police were on their way and wanted to interview him about the death of Gwendoline Warren. He told them, 'I know the woman and used to live with her, but they don't expect I did that.' At the police station he made another remark that was to ensure his arrest as soon as the Maidenhead police officers arrived. He said to the Southend police, 'I knew she was there, but I did not do it.'

Inspector Barrett and Sergeant Burbidge arrested Hutchinson and took him into custody at Maidenhead police station to await a hearing at a special sitting of the county bench. Hutchinson said to the inspector,' I knew you would be after me, as I had been in the house with her.'

The afternoon of Friday, 16th September was to see the inquest on Gwendoline Warren opened and adjoined for six weeks and Ernest Hutchinson brought before a hastily arranged police court. He was charged with murdering Mrs Gwendoline Annie Warren between 10th and 14th September. Asked by the magistrate, Lieut-Col. Simpson, DSO, if he had anything to say, Hutchinson replied, 'All I say is I am not guilty. That is all.' He was remanded in custody to Oxford gaol until the following Friday, 23rd September.

At the inquest, when invited to view the body, the jury declined, satisfied to hear an account of the deceased's physical state from the police surgeon, Dr Wilson. He had to explain that tests were currently underway in London on certain vital organs removed from Mrs Warren at the post-mortem, as it was not clear how she had met her death. The coroner, T.W. Stuchbery, said there was a good deal of mystery as to the facts. He then received evidence from Ronnie, Miss Fleet, and Joseph Hutton about their entry to the house and Hutton's grim discovery in the upstairs front bedroom. Hutton also told the coroner that he had had about an hour's conversation with Mrs Warren the previous Saturday evening. During that conversation she had indicated to Hutton that she was worried about going to bed that evening but did not say why that was. She said goodnight to Hutton about 9.15 pm. The next morning, Sunday, 11th September, Hutton saw Hutchinson in the garden, and so he asked after Gwendoline's health. Hutchinson said, 'She's in bed.'

Hutton commented, 'I suppose she is making a day of it.' Hutchinson said, 'I suppose so.'

Formal identification of the body had been carried out by Mrs Warren's estranged husband, Thomas William Warren. He confirmed that Ronnie was not his lad but he had taken on the role of father to him and his elder sister Marjorie, who had since left home. He said Mrs Warren had first left him on 5th July, 1930, to live with Hutchinson in Heywood Park, but came back to the marital home after a month or so. Their youngest daughter Connie was born in April 1931, whilst they were repairing the marriage split. It did not work, however, and she left him for good in July that year to live with Hutchinson. Mr Warren said he did not actually know the address she had moved to until he saw it on a blotting pad in the house.

So who did murder Gwendoline Warren? Her husband perhaps, who had lost her to another man and who had recently discovered her new address? Or the new man in her life, Ernest Hutchinson? What could be his motive? Perhaps neither had done it. Was there another man in Gwendoline's life, yet to be revealed? True, Hutchinson had been charged, but there was no evidence against him except he was absent from the crime scene and the most likely suspect. He had said he did not do it. It depended on the police to get to the truth of what the papers were now calling 'The Heywood Park Tragedy' and 'The Maidenhead Murder'.

With local headlines like 'Grim Discovery at Maidenhead – Woman's Body Under Mattress – Not Seen for Several Days', public interest in the case of Gwendoline Warren ran high. By the time Hutchinson was due back in Maidenhead Police Court on Friday, 23rd September, crowds of people were struggling to get inside the public gallery.

Local reports wrote how Ernest Hutchinson seemed at ease and how he carried himself in a brisk, smart manner. The hearing, which lasted only around two minutes, led to a further week's remand in custody. Hutchinson took the opportunity to seek legal aid, but he was advised that this was not the appropriate time. His next appearance at Maidenhead county bench, on Tuesday, 4th October, would be the one that would finally commit him for trial at the Berkshire Assizes in Reading, the following Thursday, 13th October.

At this last Maidenhead appearance, the public gallery was packed to capacity with crowds waiting outside to hear the details of how Mrs Warren died and what Hutchinson would say in his defence. As soon as he was charged, he replied, 'I reserve my defence. I am not guilty.'

By this time, Dr Wilson and Sir Bernard Spilsbury had been able to establish that Mrs Warren had been struck around the head with a blunt instrument, which stunned her. It was then, whilst still alive, she had been suffocated by all of the bedding and bedstead items, weighing 1 cwt 29 lbs, bearing down on her face and body. It was a chilling moment when it was revealed that in Ronnie's bedroom, under the discarded bedclothes noted by Miss Fleet when she was looking around the house with Ronnie, Dr Wilson had discovered a hammer which he said fitted the description of the blunt instrument used to attack Mrs Warren. Ronnie's bed had been taken into the spare room to be used as a deadly weight to suffocate his own mother whilst she was still alive. It was suspected, but not yet proven, that Ronnie's mother had been murdered sometime on the night of Saturday, 10th September or on the morning of Sunday, 11th.

The horror of this meant that Ronnnie, distressed and crying for his mother, who he had been told was in Birmingham, shared his mother's bed with his adopted father that Sunday night, whilst all the time his mother was lying dead in the adjoining room. Baby

Connie had also been there the whole time, in her cot at the time of the murder.

Did Ernest Hutchinson kill the mother of these two children? In searching the house, Inspector Barrett had discovered 21 letters and cards addressed to Mrs Warren from her real husband, Thomas Warren. Was there still a liaison here that led to his entering the house and murdering his wife? Was the wrong man in the dock? It seemed unlikely, but Ernest Hutchinson thought he could prove otherwise. It would be a long week until the murder trial, the media building up the tension of 'The Heywood Park Tragedy'. Tuesday, 13th October, saw the largest crowds for many years attempting to enter the Crown Court at Reading Assizes. Would he change his plea? What would be his defence? The anticipation was palpable.

Prosecuting was W.G. Earengey, KC, and with Thomas Hutchinson's defence team were Mr Micklethwait, KC and Mr Coburn. The presiding judge was Mr Justice MacKinnon.

Hutchinson had not changed his plea and he seemed relaxed and confident as he pleaded 'Not guilty' to the wilful murder of Gwendoline Annie Warren some time between 10th September and 14th September, 1932. What, of course, was going to be new was the response of Hutchinson's defence to the damning revelation that put him in the house at the time of the murder. He had already admitted to the Southend police, 'I knew she was there, but I did not do it.' Also, why was he in Southend at all, and with another woman?

First, the evidence of how the body was discovered by Mr Hutton after Miss Fleet and Ronnie had searched the house in vain, was clear enough, the horror of his find not diminished by the many occasions on which it had been retold since that fateful day. His conversation with Hutchinson over the garden fence the previous Sunday, when Hutchinson had said she was still in bed, revealed a grim truth: she was in bed, but now we know why.

The significance of Miss Fleet having noticed that the piano and other items of furniture were missing from the house was also explained. Hutchinson had been into Maidenhead, whilst Mrs Warren lay dead in the spare room, and invited Albert Davis, a second-hand furniture dealer in Bridge Street, to buy certain items, which he removed the following day. The neighbours, Mr and Mrs

Hutton had both noticed Mr Davis at the house and were told by Hutchinson that Mrs Warren had gone to Birmingham, and that he was selling some furniture to raise rent money. Mr Davis confirmed he paid Hutchinson £3.16 shillings for a piano, a small table, and a sofa, and collected them from the house, as agreed, on the day Mrs Warren's body was discovered.

Very important to the prosecution was evidence from William Miles, who lived at number 7, which shared a party wall with number 8, where Mrs Warren was murdered. He gave evidence that on the night of 10th September, around 11 pm, he heard angry voices, 'like a tiff'. When this stopped, he then heard a scraping noise, 'as if a chair was being dragged along the floor'. Mr Earengey, for the prosecution, suggested that 'the scraping noise might have been caused by a person moving a bed over another bed'.

The evidence began to mount as the testimony from the prosecution witnesses fleshed out this complex jigsaw puzzle, revealing Hutchinson as a liar engaged in the cover up of a murder he knew had taken place. He stayed in that house with the corpse of his partner for four days before disappearing, only to be discovered with another woman. It was very important now to reveal why Hutchinson was in Southend with Doris Dew. Why did he fail to go to the police if he did not murder Mrs Warren, and, if he did not do it, who did?

Doris Dew, lived in London, at 1 Oakden Street, Kensington Road. She claimed she was a domestic servant and that a girlfriend introduced her to Ernest Hutchinson at the York Hotel in Waterloo. She met him at approximately 6 pm on Wednesday, 14th September. He said his name was Ernest and he was going to Southend to check some farm stock. Doris agreed to go with him. and they booked into rooms at Broadway Market as husband and wife, Ernest, as we know, being no more a farmer than Doris was a domestic servant.

The next morning over breakfast, Doris read the newspaper and saw the description of a man wanted in connection with a murder at Maidenhead. She read it out to Hutchinson saying, 'Isn't it like you?' Hutchinson, she recalled, just said, 'Ugh.' Doris also revealed that in the attaché case mentioned in the police description were two necklaces and a yellow silk jumper, which

Hutchinson gave her as presents. These items were now identified as belonging to Mrs Warren.

Miss Dew was also able to confirm that when they met at the hotel, Hutchinson took a piece of paper from his pocket, tore a piece off, wrote his address on it and handed it to her. Doris wrote her address on the remaining piece for him to keep. The prosecution now had these two pieces of paper as evidence, for, when pieced together, they revealed on the back part of a draft letter that seemed intended for Mr Thomas Warren. It said, 'Just a few lines to you saying that the letter from Gwen is useless as I am staying at home as I won't go. I am telling you this because the baby is mine... Don't come down here under any conditions, whatever else there will be trouble . . . she is hard to get on with.' This now revealed another mystery. What was this letter from Gwen? Thomas Warren had not received a letter from his wife, nor a version of the above letter from Hutchinson advising him to ignore it. Could the letter be the key to a motive for Gwen Warren's death?

The prosecution certainly thought so, and Mr Earengay, addressing the issue of the missing letter said that it 'might suggest that on the Saturday, this woman had written to her husband as she had decided not to live with the prisoner and that, in consequence of her decision, there was a serious quarrel, which, in the end, resulted in her death'. At last it seemed that a motive had been unearthed. The lack of motive had dogged the case all along. It was now time to reveal Hutchinson's defence.

The court proceedings to date had revealed Ernest Hutchinson as not the quarrelsome kind. Neighbours said he and Gwen seemed happy enough, apart from the 'tiff' that William Miles had heard that Saturday night. Ronnie had confirmed that Ernest had been a kind father figure to him and his mother used to be worried about 'daddy' not working and the problem of finding the rent money. So it was important to the prosecution that, by peeling away the layers, he could now be seen as concealing a murder, lying about it, failing to report it to the police, dispatching the children out of the way to their auntie, and finally going off with a prostitute to Southend, where he gave her items belonging to the victim.

In his written statement made to Maidenhead police on the Friday of his arrest, he implies that someone must have got into the house and murdered Mrs Warren. He admits to having had 'sharp words' with Gwen during the afternoon. He also admits that she refused to sleep with him that night and went to the spare room, but he says, 'We were quite friendly again.' His original statement went on to say, 'I went off to sleep then, and, just after midnight or between 12 pm and 1 am, I heard someone go downstairs and guessed it was her. Some time after, I heard someone come back. I did not look out to see who it was. On Sunday morning between six and half-past, I went down to get a cup of tea – made the tea, and brought it back upstairs. I drunk some of my own and went to look for her, as I had made a cup of tea for her and some biscuits for the baby. I looked in the back room where the boy usually sleeps and did not see anyone. I then went into the spare front bedroom, and as soon as I got into the room I thought something was wrong because the bedstead and spare mattress were all put on top of this other bed. I inspected this other bed and pulled the cover up at the far end near the chimney and I could see some stockinged feet. I looked further along and I could see there was a dead woman there, which I recognized in a minute, so I simply put the things back just as I found them when I lifted the cover up, came out and shut the door.'

He said he knew Mrs Warren had received letters from her husband threatening 'that he would do all the injury he could, so I do not know whether he done it or not'. Unfortunately for Hutchinson, none of the 21 letters and cards revealed to the court by Inspector Barrett from Mr Warren contained any threats to injure her. But, of course, that did not mean they did not exist, merely they had not been found.

One of the most important arguments advanced by the prosecution was to ask how anyone else could 'have got into the house and moved the bed and bedding on top of that woman without his hearing a single thing'. In his statement, he had talked about someone going downstairs and upstairs, yet he did not hear anything that would indicate Mrs Warren was being attacked in one room, and then bedding taken from another room being piled on top of her before her attacker left the house. Hutchinson had also revealed in this statement that on the Monday, having seen Ronnie and Connie onto the bus for Farnham Common and knowing Mrs Warren was dead, 'I went back to Heywood Park and had my dinner and just messed about the house and outside until the evening. In the evening I went to the picture theatre and came out about half past nine.'

That night he said he had slept soundly at 8 Heywood Avenue. On this particular point, the judge intervened and asked Hutchinson, 'Did you sleep soundly?' Hutchinson replied, 'Yes.' Mr Justice MacKinnon then observed, 'You knew all the while that this poor woman was lying dead under all this stuff?' Hutchinson replied that he knew she was there on the Sunday morning, but did not know what to do for the best. Hutchinson even claimed he did actually set off to tell the police, borrowing a bike from William Miles at number 7 to do so, but got as far as Taplow, remembered he had left the baby alone, and so went back to the house. Mr Miles confirmed Hutchinson had borrowed his bike on Sunday morning in a vain attempt to cycle to Birmingham to see Mrs Warren but claimed he'd only got as far as Taplow and turned back.

The prosecution had made the point very forcibly: 'Here was a women with whom he had been living on affectionate terms for some months, dead in the house, but he did not know what to do. An ordinary person would have rushed immediately to the police. Instead of that the accused told a neighbour that his wife had gone to Birmingham.'

'Why didn't you go to the police?' Mr Earengey asked Hutchinson.

'I was upset,' said Hutchinson.

At this reply, Justice McKinnon, seeming perhaps less neutral than he should have been, interjected, commenting, 'Were you so upset that you could sell her furniture and pick up a prostitute in London?' Hutchinson remained silent.

Earengey asked once more, 'Why didn't you tell the police?'

'Because it's the police's duty to find out their own jobs. I am not a lover of the police,' said Hutchinson. This was hardly a reply calculated to enhance his defence.

The trial concluded on Saturday, 15th October. Given the evidence to date, the position for Messrs Micklethwait and Coburn was a difficult one. When Mr Coburn for the defence asked Hutchinson whether he had murdered Mrs Warren, 'No' was the direct and clear answer. Mr Micklethwait claimed that the

THE MAIDENHEAD ADVERTISER, WEDNESDAY,

# FIGHT FOR A LIFE.

## The Discovery of a Woman's Body under a Pile of Mattresses

## In a Semi-Detached House at Heywood Park.

## Accused Man on his Trial at the Berks Assize.

## Prisoner Sentenced to Death.

Headline from the *Maidenhead Advertiser*, dated 19th October, 1932.

prosecution had not satisfied the court that the murder actually took place in that house. Nor had they satisfied the court that it was Hutchinson who attacked her. If it did not take place in there, it would explain away the prosecution's point that when Mr Miles, who lived next door, heard a scraping noise, Hutchinson was bound to have heard the attack on his wife but did not. Someone else could have done it, but elsewhere! For the jury, this was opening up an enormous credibility gap

Mr Micklethwaith struggled on vainly. He put it to the jury that it was also possible that a tussle took place with someone, during which Mrs Warren fell, and that is how she died. He said no motive for murder had been revealed. Also, he reminded the jury that they were not there to try Hutchinson for being a liar or a coward. The prosecution's job was to show, beyond reasonable doubt, that he murdered Gwendoline Annie Warren, and, in his opinion, they had not done so. Would this also be the jury's opinion?

After the judge's summing up, in which he said there was no doubt Mrs. Warren was murdered some time during 10th or 11th

September at 8 Heywood Avenue, the jury retired. They returned after 1 hour 10 minutes. It was reported that Hutchinson stepped smartly into the dock. He looked directly at Justice Mackinnon and did not glance at the jury as their foreman pronounced a verdict of guilty. The *Maidenhead Chronicle* reported this final part of the murder trial thus:

> 'Hutchinson's lips twitched as the black cap was placed on Mr Justice MacKinnon's head and when his Lordship, in a broken voice, pronounced the death sentence, he [Hutchinson] smiled and then broke into a mirthless laugh. He turned, and stepped smartly from the dock, a smile still on his face.'

After a failed appeal hearing on 15th November, based on the claim that Justice McKinnon misdirected the jury, Hutchinson was executed by judicial hanging on Wednesday, 23rd November at Oxford. It made but five short lines at the bottom of page 12 of the *Chronicle*, under the heading 'Maidenhead Murderer Hanged'.

It was over for Hutchinson, but a life sentence of grief for the family had begun that fateful day in September when Auntie Fleet and Ronnie visited 8 Heywood Avenue in search of the truth.

# The Mysterious Death of Lucy Gmiterek

*'Here is a small burnt patch of flooring; here is the tinder from a little bundle of burnt paper, but not so light as usual, seeming to be steeped in something; and here is – is it the cinder of a small charred and broken leg of wood sprinkled with white ashes, or is it coal? O Horror, he is here! and this from which we run away, striking out the light and overturning one another into the street, is all that represents him.'*

Description of the burnt remains of Krook, who died by spontaneous combustion:
Charles Dickens, *Bleak House*, 1852–3

Certain mysteries continue to be researched but constantly elude explanation, or at least an explanation that all can agree upon. One such very frightening mystery is that of spontaneous human combustion. The very idea that, without warning, a human being can burst into flames and die as a result is not something we care to think about, but such cases do happen. Indeed, it was said to have happened to Mrs Lucy Gmiterek on Sunday, 12th November, 1978 at her Baker Street home in Reading, Berkshire.

Before we look at the tragic death of Mrs Gmiterek, we need to know why this death, and others like it, was classified as spontaneous human combustion and how this can be identified as such. When Charles Dickens killed his character Krook in *Bleak House*, he created a great deal of controversy when he claimed it was caused by spontaneous combustion. But, by the time Dickens used this as a fictional occurrence, he was aware of upwards of 30 such cases having been documented since the 17th century. There have, of course, been many hundreds of such incidents reported since Dickens' time.

The *British Medical Journal* of 1905, which reported on the death of an elderly woman in similar circumstances to the case of Mrs Gmiterek, described the scene as follows:

'A small pyramidal heap of broken calcinated human bones, on the top of which was a skull, on the floor in front of a chair. All the bones were completely bleached and brittle; every particle of soft-tissue had been consumed, and yet a tablecloth within three feet of the remains was not even scorched.'

The body, therefore, is usually much more severely burned than would occur during a 'normal' fire. The mysterious facts of such episodes provide a picture of heat more intense than any crematorium – some 3000 degrees Fahrenheit – yet it is so localized that easily inflammable objects in very close proximity to the body are not damaged. (In fact crematoria will operate at only 2000 degrees Fahrenheit, which leaves bone fragments which then have to be ground up by hand.)

Sometimes the poor person finding such a scene will be confronted with the charred remains of the person except for small portions of the body (a foot or an arm, possibly the head) that remain unburnt. Most mysterious of all, calcined bones can, on occasions, be found inside unburnt clothes. A greasy sooty deposit emanating from the burning flesh can cover the ceiling and walls, usually stopping three to four feet above the floor. Also, it has happened that people in an adjoining room to the tragedy have heard no screams of pain or cries for help. It is thought that the event is so rapid and so intense that the victim has no chance even to call out. The source of the fire appears to be internal: burning from the inside out. Is this what happened to Mrs Lucy Gmiterek on that tragic November day at her Baker Street home in Reading?

That morning, Mrs Elizabeth Randall had heard someone hammering on her front door, someone in a panic. When she opened it, it was her neighbour's 8-year-old daughter, Maria Gmiterek. She was in a very distressed state and, between crying

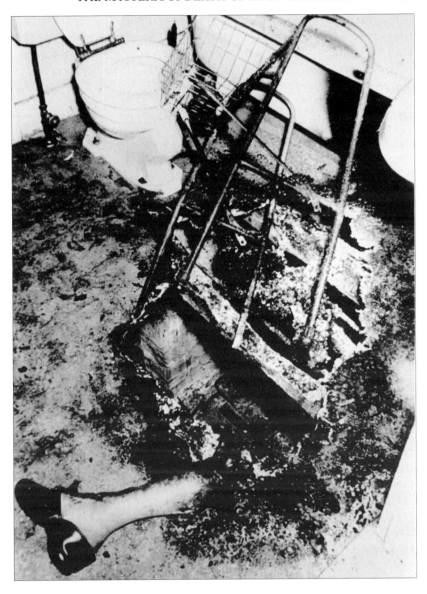

Spontaneous human combustion can destroy the whole body, just leaving part of a limb intact, as in the case of another victim (shown above) who appeared to have suffered this fate in 1966. (© Fortean Picture Library)

and sobbing, managed to tell Mrs Randall that something had happened to her mother.

Mrs Randall ran next door and as soon as she got into the house she smelled burning. Maria led her to the basement, where the burning smell was quite intense, and there lying on the floor was the badly charred body of her widowed neighbour Mrs Lucy Gmiterek. Her distressed daughter cried out to Mrs Randall, 'Is my Mummy dead? My Mummy has turned to ashes.'

Maria's brother, 11-year-old Peter, came downstairs to see what was going on. Mrs Randall quickly sent him across the road to a house where they had a telephone, with instructions to call an ambulance. Meanwhile, she took Maria back to her house to care for her. Peter returned and tried to comfort his distressed sister while they all waited for the ambulance to arrive. Mrs Randall is reported as saying at the time, 'Peter was trying to be very grown up, trying to help, but the little girl was heartbroken. It was terrible in that basement. I don't want to see anything like that again. It's bad enough for an adult to see, but imagine what it must be like for a child to find her mother like that.'

A post-mortem was held the following morning at the Royal Berkshire Hospital.

The shock to 49-year-old Mrs Gmiterek's nervous system caused by extensive burning was said to be the cause of death rather than the burning itself. The remainder of the room showed such little fire damage, police and fire experts could not explain why.

'BLAZE DEATH RIDDLE' headlined the *Reading Chronicle*, 'Forensic scientists were still trying to solve the mysterious death of a Reading mother in a fire at her home on Sunday . . . police and fire experts are known to be puzzled why Mrs Gmiterek should have burned to death while the rest of the room was barely damaged by flames.'

Her doctor, Rojand Shukla, gave evidence at the inquest about Mrs Gmiterek's acute back pains, for which he could find no explanation, and she had begun to find herself shaking so much that sometimes she could not stand. Did she perhaps knock over an oil fire whilst trying to do some washing in the basement area? This was the supposition by the fire and forensic experts. However, they could find no evidence of this.

Why did Lucy Gmiterek burn to death whilst the rest of the

room was barely touched by fire? To cause the charing of her body, it must have taken a temperature of over 2000 degrees Farenheit, which should have severely damaged the house. Explanations for this situation continue to baffle the experts, who struggle to find rational, scientific explanations.

It was thought for a long time that the victims of this kind of burning were alcoholics, so soaked in crude alcohol that any spark would ignite their bodies. This has been shown not to be a valid explanation, particularly as many victims were teetotallers. It is also impossible to burn alcohol-soaked flesh at the temperatures required for this sort of combustion Other theories relate to flammable body fat, but many victims can be elderly and quite frail.

Can people literally short-circuit in some way? Does some form of internal reaction, whether from natural chemicals or diet, generate heat and then rapid, spontaneous burning from within: almost a freak form of microwave oven, i.e. cooking from the inside out?

It seems that there is still no satisfactory explanation of the occurrences known as spontaneous human combustion and so Lucy Gmiterek's death also remains a mystery.

# EVIL DEEDS AT WATCHFIELD

*'See how love and murder will out'*
William Congreve (1670-1729): *The Double Dealer*

The stench of the black smoke billowing out from the cottage opposite was acrid and unbearable, and Ann Butler could stand it no longer. It was an early evening on a warm July day and all her cottage windows had to be kept closed to keep the offensive smell from completely taking over. The thick smoke with a peculiar smell was pouring not only from the chimney but curling out from under the roof tiles of the wash house attached to the Carters' cottage across the road. We are in the tiny old Berkshire hamlet of Watchfield and the date is Friday, 21st July, 1893.

The cottage in question was the home of John and Rhoda Carter and their two sons, Thomas, aged nine, and William, nearly three. The Carters had not been married very long, Thomas being John's son from a previous marriage. John also had three daughters from a marriage before that: Martha, aged 15, who was living away and working in service, Clara, 17, making her own way in the world somewhere, and Annie 16, also living away in service.

John Carter, now 40, had been unfortunate in that his first wife had fallen downstairs and broken her neck some years ago, when he lived near Longcot. Villagers were very sorry for him losing the wife he loved and having to bring up three baby daughters on his own. John soon met and married his second wife, but unfortunately she mysteriously disappeared: 'Ran off and left us,' John told concerned folk. Now he was happily married again, to Rhoda, aged 30; had another son, William; and was working hard as an agricultural labourer on the small farm to which the cottage was attached.

Country folk like Ann were used to the odours of boiling offal from the farm, and the distinctive smell of home-made glue bubbling in the farmhouse smithy, also across the road, but this pollution from the cottage wash house was too much to bear. She waited a little longer, but by seven o'clock enough was enough. She went across the road and, looking in the open door, saw a tub standing on the ground and a coal fire around it, billowing smoke. John was poking the coals and was barely visible in the haze. She asked what he was up to, and he said he was just burning some old rubbish, nothing to worry about. She asked where Rhoda was and the children. The children were in the house, he said, and Rhoda had gone to Eastleach to see her sister.

John Carter didn't know that Ann Butler already knew that Rhoda was supposed to have gone off to Eastleach, where she had a pregnant sister, Jane, about to be confined. Only the day before, she had been talking to Rhoda's mother, who lived in a cottage about 30 yards from her daughter and son-in-law. Her name was Mrs Titcomb and she was worried stiff about the whereabouts of her daughter. Mrs Titcomb had told Ann that when she called to visit Rhoda around midday yesterday she wasn't there, and John had told her she had gone to Eastleach to look after Jane. 'What, without coming to see me?' Mrs Titcomb had asked. 'Without saying anything to me about it?' Ann agreed it was odd that she would go off like that without telling her mother. What made it even more strange, Mrs Titcomb had confided, was that Rhoda left at the crack of dawn, at milking time, around 4.30 am.

Another thing that Rhoda's mother could not understand was that the previous evening, about eight or nine o'clock, she had seen her daughter and son-in-law strolling back to the cottage and had bade them good night. 'Why didn't she say anything to to me then?' she had asked John. He had told her that, when they got indoors, Rhoda had said her face was burning, which meant that somebody wanted to see her and that it would be her sister Jane. She decided she would get up early in the morning when he went to milk the cows and get to Eastleach in good time to assist her sister's confinement.

Recalling this conversation with Rhoda's mother, Ann suddenly heard herself saying to John Carter, 'It's all wrong.' She found herself blurting out 'Have you murdered Rhoda?' John did not get angry. He just did not reply, but looked at her in a frightening way. Ann Butler left and watched him from her cottage. She saw him go back and forth two or three times to the pump for pails of water, the smoke continuing to pour from the wash house over the next hour or so.

She then saw a man approaching. It was Rhoda's brother, David, who lived with his parents. He stood watching the smoke billowing out. The wash house door was now tight shut. He tried lifting the latch, but it was so hot it burnt his fingers. At that moment John Carter came round from the corner of the house, walked straight past David as if he didn't exist, lifted the latch and went in. David followed him.

Inside it was dense with smoke, and he could barely see. It wasn't possible to make out what was burning other than coals, which he could see glowing here and there. It was dark with acrid smoke and he warned John he was in danger of burning down the cottage. Carter said he could throw some water on the fire, which he did, causing even more smoke to rise from the hissing coals.

David asked his brother-in-law what on earth he was doing with this large fire in the wash house. John merely told him he was boiling some water to shave with. He didn't seem in the mood to discuss it any further; so David continued to assist in putting out the fire. The smoke began to diminish and slowly fade. The smell, however, hung in the air. David said goodnight and went home to tell his mother that John insisted Rhoda was with Jane at Eastleach, but he was not convinced.

An uneasy atmosphere now existed between John and his mother-in-law, who wanted to come into the cottage to tidy and see exactly how it had been left. Carter kept himself to himself over the weekend, the eldest son, Thomas, assisting with duties around the farm. His father had explained that his mother had gone to visit his auntie, but he never knew he had an Auntie Jane. John told his son that if anyone asked where his mother was, he was to say he didn't know. William was also missing his mother, but was being lovingly cared for by his big brother, Tom.

What was worrying young Tom was the memory of the last time he had heard his mother's voice. It had seemed distressed. On the previous Thursday evening, when his granny had seen her daughter and son-in-law heading back to the cottage and bade them good-night, Tom was asleep upstairs. He had stayed up quite late and seen his father and stepmother set off, but had fallen asleep waiting for them to return. His little brother was fast asleep in the same bed. Suddenly, during the night, he had been woken up by a noise from his parents' bedroom. It was a heavy, clumping noise that went on for ten minutes or so. It then seemed to move down the stairs, and he heard his mother's voice saying 'Lord have mercy on us.' Then there was a kind of rolling noise. He tried to keep awake to listen some more but fell asleep. It was around 4 am the next morning, when his father had woken him to milk the cows, that he discovered his mother was not in the house. Whilst he was milking the cows, his father took a fork and shovel and told him he was going off to make a trench in the blacksmith's shop. This took him about fifteen minutes, after which he prepared breakfast, and called Tom inside.

Tom's mother would normally have got the breakfast and washed and dressed his little brother. Now his mother was gone, his father was getting breakfast, and he had to wash and dress his brother. It was very unsettling. His father also told him not to use the wash house and not to go upstairs that day. Of course, his granny didn't know all this, and Tom had no one except his dad to turn to – and he was not a demonstrative man.

On Saturday, 22nd July, the village gossip was of nothing else except the sudden disappearance of Rhoda Carter. Mrs Titcomb was very distressed. There had been no word from her other daughter Jane at Eastleach about Rhoda arriving there. Mrs Titcomb went to visit PC Sparks, whom she'd know for years, and told him of her fears. He was already aware of the gossip; it was a tiny village and this kind of news spread rapidly. Around 11 o'clock that evening, he called at John Carter's cottage and was invited in. He asked Carter about the report circulating in the village that something serious had happened between them. Carter said, 'There's nothing in it. She has gone to Eastleach to her sister's. We went out for a walk on Thursday night last and when we returned she said she would like to have her sister here for her confinement. I said I am not going to have her here. I married you to look after me and my children, not your sister. She said she should go to Eastleach, and I then said if she went she could stop there and don't come back here again. She started for Eastleach early the next morning and I left the house soon afterwards and hung the key up in the blacksmith's shop.'

PC Sparks listened carefully, and left.

The gossip intensified on Sunday, and, by Monday, Rhoda's mother could stand it no more. Around midday she went to the cottage, where she saw her son-in-law in the garden. She asked to go upstairs to make the beds and open the windows and tidy up whilst her daughter was away. John Carter refused and said he would see to it presently. Mrs Titcomb left, unhappy, and determined to find out what was going on in the house. She did go back about three o'clock that same day and managed to slip upstairs. There she saw her daughter's clothes in the bedroom. The sort of clothes she would have worn to travel to Eastleach and stay with her sister. Missing were the clothes she was wearing that Thursday evening when she said goodnight to them both: a mackintosh, an old pair of boots, and a black hat.

Rhoda's mother was distressed. She felt very strongly that that she would never see her daughter again. She told PC Sparks about the clothing left behind, and he decided to accompany Mrs Titcomb back to her daughter's cottage. They found Carter on the farm and went with him back to the house. Mrs Titcomb pointed out her daughter's hat and jacket and linen underwear, which she would have been wearing for any journey when she was intending to stay away. PC Sparks said to Carter, 'What clothes was your wife wearing when she was sitting at breakfast on Friday morning?' Of course, like Tom, we know Rhoda was not there for breakfast – it was a good question!

Before Carter answered, PC Sparks felt there were enough suspicious circumstances to caution him. Carter said, 'She was wearing a black jacket, a dark linsey dress, a pair of old shoes, and a black straw hat.' Whilst Carter spoke, PC Sparks studied a deep scratch on the suspect's cheek. His next question was to ask him how it happened. Carter said that the cows had been escaping through a gap in the cow house, so he got a bush and wedged it into the gap when a bough flew up and scratched his face.

PC Sparks and Mrs Titcomb left the cottage, Sparks promising he would make further inquiries at Eastleach. In fact he knew already that Rhoda had never got as far as her sister's: discreet inquiries had already been made. He suspected foul play and needed a reason to search the whole house and farm area, but he was careful not to alarm Mrs Titcomb unnecessarily.

The next day, Tuesday, 25th July, something quite unexpected happened: James Carter, John's brother, who lived at Shrivenham, met up with John walking by Pennyhook's Meadows, about a quarter of a mile outside Watchfield. James asked what he'd been up to, and John's reply was direct: 'I have killed my wife.' James was horrified and asked what he had done to her. His brother said he had hit her with one blow and killed her, dragged her to the blacksmith's shop and buried her.

Carter begged his brother to go into Watchfield, find out what people suspected and report back. He would wait by the fields. James did as his brother asked and went into the village. PC Sparks noticed James asking around, watched him, and then followed him back to where John Carter was waiting and arrested him on suspicion of murdering his wife. He claimed he had been looking for her at Lechlade and Eastleach. PC Sparks did not accept his story and took him into custody.

Watchfield was buzzing with the news of Carter's arrest. Mrs Titcomb had care of her grandchildren, and, at 9 pm on Wednesday, 26th July, almost a week after Rhoda Carter had last been seen alive, the police arrived to search the family home. They saw the remnants of a fire in the wash house, but no sign of Mrs Carter or bodily remains. PC Sparks and PC Benning went to the blacksmith's shop and, armed with an iron bar, probed the earthen floor. It was a rough surface, compacted by years of work and covered with stones and litter. However, in one corner was a large wheelbarrow and under it was a big wooden tile. They removed both objects to probe the earth, when they touched something soft. They scrabbled at the earth, and, only three inches down, they found the body of a woman.

Rhoda was lying on her right side with her head doubled right down to her knees. She was wearing just a chemise. The police officers carefully lifted the body onto a plank and carried it into the wash house, where they could lay it out ready for the police surgeon. Lots of hair fell away from her as if her scalp had been scalded. They noticed there was a black mark about four inches along her throat, and her nose was completely smashed in and dislocated.

Mr Spackman, the doctor, arrived and he noted the severe discolouring around her face, right arm, and the side of her body, and how the skin just flaked and peeled off as if it had been boiled. He said the discolouration of the face was mainly due to being constantly beaten by a hand or flat object. He could not say if that had occurred before or after death. Decomposition had set in and so there was also skin discolouration resulting from the natural processes of decay.

Clearly visible on her throat were three distinct marks: one on the right side corresponding with the pressure of the thumb and two on the left corresponding with the pressure of two fingers. As a result of this, her thyroid gland had been dislocated. Strangulation was definitely the cause of death. Regarding her smashed nose, he could not tell if this had been carried out before or after death. He thought it was either pummeled or more likely, stamped on with a heavy boot. The body was later further examined by Mr T. Bond of Westminster Hospital, who agreed fully with Mr Spackman's analysis. They also agreed that, despite the rather overpowering smell of putrifaction, there was also a burning smell on the body; so someone had tried to burn it, but unsuccessfully.

In the wash house the police raked through the fire and discovered burnt buttons and stays. In the house they discovered a blood-stained blanket on the couch and a shirt that smelt of burning, also with blood stains.

## SHOCKING WIFE MURDER IN BERKSHIRE
## THE BODY FOUND UNDER AN EARTHEN FLOOR

The *Reading Observer* for Saturday, 29th July pulled no punches. It went on to describe 'the almost naked corpse being blackened and scarred'. Watchfield was on the murder map and was guaranteed a weekend and more of sightseers from all over the county to gaze in awe at the scene of the crime. How distressing this must have been for Rhoda's mother and her grandchildren.

This horrendous murder led the newspaper to consider the fact that John Carter had been married three times. Could we be sure that his first wife was killed in an accident and his second wife had run away? They had been tipped off about the possibility he may be a serial killer, and, on that same Saturday, they felt confident enough to run a piece entitled *Mystery about Carter's other Wives*, in which was written: 'The reason of the popular excitement which was not alluded to at the inquest lies in the mysterious fate of Carter's two previous wives, he having been twice previously married. The first died from falling downstairs and breaking her neck, but it is now being recalled that it was upon Carter's sole evidence that the verdict of 'accidental death' was returned by the coroner's jury. He was regarded as a respectable man and no shadow of suspicion was attached to her death until this murder was brought to light. His second wife mysteriously disappeared three years ago, but a villager says she is still alive.' Was she still alive? No one had seen her since Carter claimed she 'ran off'.

The trial was set for the Berkshire autumn assizes. Meanwhile, the police had no means of re-examining the case of his first wife. The verdict of accidental death would have to stand. They did, however, intend to try and find out what really happened to his second wife and to resolve that mystery once and for all. Was she still alive, or did Carter murder her too?

Carter's trial for the wilful murder of Rhoda Ann Carter took place on Thursday, 16th November under Mr Justice Cave. For the prosecution were Mr Darling and Mr Daniel, and for the defence, Mr McCarthy and Mr Sherwood. John Carter's plea was 'Not guilty'.

It was clear that the evidence against him was overwhelming. His confession to his brother was unambiguous. To a packed courtroom, the whole story unfolded, showing how he had carried out the most horrendous violence upon his wife. Even his son James, aged 9, was called to give evidence. It was James who had been sent by his father to get coal to bring to the wash house, in a bizarre attempt to destroy his mother's body by boiling it in water. He recalled how his father made him promise him not to go into the wash house and not to discuss where his mother had gone.

To a hushed court he described how, that fateful night, he had heard the heavy clumping noise from his bedroom and his mother's voice crying out.

As the witnesses told their tales, the defence, on cross-examination, asked each of them whether they thought John and Rhoda were happy. Not one prosecution witness described them as anything but a happily married couple. No motive at all was emerging. Why did he do it? Was it as simple as an argument over Rhoda wanting her sister to come and stay? No one knows what was said on that Thursday evening walk, or in the house afterwards. Whatever it was, why did it lead to murder?

It was clear that the defence hoped that with no evidence of motive, they might manage to convince a jury it was manslaughter and avoid the gallows for their client. But, for a charge of manslaughter, there has to be some form of 'reasonable' provocation that drove the person to kill. No provocation appeared to have come from Rhoda that night to make John kill her, bury her, and try to boil her body. One insight into John's mind came from Lucy Carter, his brother's wife, who recalled an incident on Friday, 7th June. She told of meeting Rhoda and John as they were going home from the Watchfield Club Feast. She said Rhoda was hanging her head and looked unhappy and would not speak to her. A few days later, she met John by his cottage, and asked him why Rhoda was unhappy coming home from the feast. He said, 'She wanted to dance and I told her she might dance with a female but not with a man, as if I thought she wanted another man I would be the death of her.'

Was this a man of intense jealously: jealous if she danced with another man on a local feast day; jealous if she gave attention to her pregnant sister? Could his motivation have been as basic as a destructive, selfish jealously? The defence could ask very little of the jury, as they could not find any witnesses that could provide reasons to consider a verdict of manslaughter rather than murder. Their closing speech merely reminded the jury that 'if they were not satisfied that there were circumstances reducing the crime to manslaughter, then they must do their duty to their country and find that verdict which their reason and common sense might dictate to them'.

In fact, the jury pondered only a matter of minutes and did not

The village of Watchfield still retains its 19th-century character.

even wish to leave their places in the court room. The verdict was 'Guilty as charged'.

When the judge placed the black cap on his head in readiness to pronounce the death sentence, he alluded to the puzzle everyone was left with: why did he do it? He said, 'What happened between you and that unfortunate woman on the night in question, no one but you and your Maker know, but that you killed her there can be no doubt whatsoever.' John Carter remained unmoved as the judge went on to say, 'You have offended the laws of your country by taking the life of her whom you were bound to cherish and protect and for that I have no choice but to pass sentence upon you.'

The custom at that time was that, once the death sentence was pronounced, three Sundays would be allowed to pass and then the execution would be carried out. Would this time yield up a full confession and still the now rampant gossip and newspaper speculation about the fate of Carter's previous wives? In the event, the law gave Carter an extra fourth Sunday before his execution, which was scheduled for Tuesday, 5th December, at 8 am.

Rumours that he had confessed to murdering his other wives were rife, but the newspapers had no real evidence of this, and the reading public awaited the reports of his execution with anticipation. But, the governor of Reading gaol, in a very controversial move, decided not to allow the press to witness and report on the execution of John Carter. Representatives of the press were seething. The much awaited last minute salving of conscience often happens at the scaffold, and it was their job to report it to the masses. They claimed it was, in fact, their moral duty to report on the execution of convicted murderers, as well as a long tradition. The newspapers were also not going to be told if he had made a confession of his guilt to the prison chaplain.

In an angry editorial, the *Reading Observer* commented, 'What possible harm could follow if it were officially made known that the convict had made a confession of his guilt? It would relieve the minds of those on whom the responsibility of his conviction had fallen and would also put an end to idle rumours, which may or may not have a basis in truth. Publicity may aid in the prevention of crime, whilst, so far as we can see, nothing is gained by secrecy.' It was a mystery that the governor should act in this manner. Nevertheless, Carter was executed within the confines the Reading gaol as scheduled, without any representatives of the press as witnesses.

However, the tale of John Carter is not quite over. The police were determined to solve the mystery of the missing second wife and had been working hard in the meantime to find her, and find her they did. Her skeleton was discovered buried in a ditch at Faringdon, near the corner of a field on Broadleaze Farm, where Carter used to work as a labourer. So, ten days after his execution, an inquest jury sitting at the Barrington Arms Hotel in Shrivenham on Friday, 15th December, 1893 heard the disturbing truth about the fate of John Carter's second wife. The story came from Martha, one of John Carter's daughters from his first marriage. Martha may well have long suspected that her father killed her birth mother by throwing her downstairs and breaking her neck, and now she had no doubt that her father did kill her stepmother. Her remembrance was so similar to that told by her 9-year-old stepbrother James at Carter's trial.

Martha, then aged 12 and living with her sisters and

stepbrother, father and stepmother at Faringdon, had been awakened about eight or nine at night by what she thought were falling chairs. When she got up at about 6.30 am her father had gone to work, and there was no sign of her stepmother. When her father came back for breakfast at about 8 o'clock, he asked Martha were her mother was. He was quite normal asking this question, and Martha said she did not know. He said without hesitating, 'She's run away then.' He promised to look for her down at Longcot. Martha recalled an argument between her father and stepmother the night before her stepmother disappeared. He gave her 24 shillings, saying it was all his wages for two weeks' work, and she said it was not enough and threw it back at him.

Two or three months after her stepmother's disappearance, they moved to Watchfield, and Martha left home to work in service. About three months after that, she confronted her father one day when she visited him at Watchfield and said to him, 'What do you think Clara told me?' John Carter replied, 'I don't know.' Martha continued, 'She told me that you said you killed stepmother and buried her in the Faringdon Road ditch. Is this true?' John Carter, said it was an accident, he had just knocked her on the forehead.

It was becoming clear to all concerned that Carter had been a seriously violent man with no motive to kill other than to vent his own implacable anger at some trivial domestic matter. Despite the reluctance of the governor at Reading prison to discuss whether or not Carter had confessed, it was clear from the inquest that the Revd Martin Thomas Friend, the chaplain of Reading prison, had felt it his duty to let the authorities know that Carter had told him he had buried the body of his second wife at the place where it had since been found. Carter told the chaplain he wanted her to have a decent burial and end the speculation that anyone else was implicated in her death.

So, there was a confession of sorts, and had the chaplain kept it to himself, the mystery of Carter's second wife may never have been solved. Once more, a jury was to return a verdict of murder against John Carter. More the pity, thought many, that he couldn't be executed again, and then once more, so each of his three wives could be avenged for his brutal actions.

# THE READING POLTERGEIST

*'It has long been held that at the centre of any poltergeist activity will be found a disturbed adolescent girl. But experts now believe that sexual tension in young or old, male or female, may cause the phenomenon.'*
Marvels and Mysteries: Ghosts, Orbis Publishing, 1995

When someone talks about ghosts or hauntings, it is usual to be a little sceptical, to be cautious about whether such entities really exist. It is also quite common to picture ghostly white beings floating through solid objects such as doors and walls. But as paranormal investigators will testify, this is not what being haunted generally means. In the early stages of what may be termed paranormal activity, it could be a strange odour, perhaps a footstep or two where there should not be any at all, possibly a cold spot in a centrally heated room that just lingers. Pet dogs or cats may suddenly flee a room or refuse to enter it altogether. The most difficult to explain is a feeling of being watched, and not all will feel the same pair of watching eyes, if they are, in fact, eyes! Welcome to level 1 of playing host to a poltergeist; you only have four more levels to go before all hell breaks loose.

This is what happened to Mrs Adams, an elderly Reading resident and her daughter, Pauline, over an 18-month period beginning at the end of 1979.

The term *poltergeist* is of German origin and literally translates

*The Five Levels of Poltergeist Activity listing: (1) Typical features of poltergeist activity to expect at each level, and (2) The Reading Poltergeist activity actually experienced by Mrs Adams, daughter Pauline, grandson Stephen, friends and visitors to their house (1979–1981).*

## Level 1: Senses Attack
(1) Cold spots, strange noises, odours and smells, hearing footsteps, household pets acting strangely, feelings of being watched, objects moving to new positions.
(2) Cold spots and breezes, smell of gas but no leaks, chairs tipped over, drawers left open, furniture moved to different rooms.

## Level 2: Visible and Audible Attack
(1) Laughing, whispering, moans, shrieks, sudden breezes, visible clouds, stange marks on walls or floors, strong static electricity, everyday objects go missing.
(2) Ceiling lights swinging, soap powder boxes dancing in mid air then contents tipped out, pairs of shoes disappear, paper money is shredded and scattered.

## Level 3: Intensified Poltergeist Activity
(1) Lights, cookers, televisions, etc. turned off and on, feelings of being touched, punched or grabbed, writing on walls, doors and floors, hearing complete words, seeing apparitions, strange telephone calls.
(2) Clocks starting and stopping throughout the house, gas leak smells continue – no cause found, water leaks start – no cause found, constant debris to clear up from broken household objects.

## Level 4: Poltergeist Gathers Momentum – Dangerous Period for Possible Personal Injury
(1) Flying objects such as ornaments and crockery. Objects disappear and reappear elsewhere, furniture shakes, fires suddenly start, physical pushing felt, dizzy and nauseous feelings, objects break for no reason (e.g. mirrors), levitation especially of children.
(2) Doors flung open with such force the door knob penetrates the wall, contents of kitchen cupboards disappear then reappear in the hall, occupants bombarded with china, crockery and glassware, bicycle glides up the stairs and wedges in the banisters, *Reading Evening Post* reporter chased by floating kettle, sideboard smashes into wall.

## Level 5: Poltergeist Highest Energy Point. Action needs to be taken before serious injury and even sexual assault occurs. After this level 'burns out'; the activity begins once more at Level 1 and so the cycle repeats.
(1) Biting, slapping, hair pulling, possible sexual advances, fires, blood on the walls, flying heavy or sharp objects directly at occupants or visitors. Heavy objects falling, threatening writing on walls, floors, doors.
(2) Broom shoots down hall through letter box and onto pavement (twice), flying medicine box hits Mrs Adams who needed stitches, grandson's clothes 'torn' from body, then dropped from mid air, pairs of missing shoes shower down from mid air, outside, house number changed from 121 to 1231, then flies off striking visitor, half pound of butter thrown at visitor.

as 'noisy spirit'. It may not be too noisy in the early stages, but, once it takes to its location and a person or people within that location, it will certainly announce its presence. Also, a poltergeist is not a ghost, although in the early stages, people would describe their experience as that of being haunted by a ghost or ghosts. Poltergeists do not have to be associated with death and dying: far from it, they tend to be associated with the young and developing. They often feed on the energy of young teenagers

However, in the Reading case we will examine, apart from a visiting grandson, there were no 'young energies' in the house. Mrs Adams was in her eighties and her daughter in her fifties. It seems such hauntings can latch onto other forms of energy we may be unaware of giving out.

In the case of older people, some paranormal investigators have claimed that poltergeist activity is associated with those in poor mental and physical health, who are perhaps vulnerable to stress. Newer claims from researchers suggest that the female connection can occur at each end of the spectrum: young girls entering puberty or older women whose metabolism is changing once more as the menopause is approaching. Both situations are felt to provide the sexual tensions thought to manifest as the paranormal experience we call a poltergeist.

It was not shown conclusively that any of these conditions fitted Mrs Adams and her daughter Pauline exactly, although it seems that it was Pauline who was most closely 'tormented' by the poltergeist, and, being in her fifties, this fitted the theory of sexual tensions or energies at the menopausal stage.

The most important difference between what may be seen as a haunting and a poltergeist is that a haunting is normally associated with a location. The poltergeist, however, connects to a person and can move wherever that person moves. Now that is very scary.

At level one, however, a haunting and a poltergeist are very similar. Even level two may not reveal the culprit, as the signs are still very ghostly, as if the presence was there solely because of the location not the person. This is the level used so much in films about hauntings – hearing whispers, children laughing when no children live in the house, perhaps moans and shrieks. Possibly there is a strong static electricity around the room and strange markings appear on the floor or walls. The poltergeist has now warmed up to level three, and the strange marks become, in parts, decipherable words, such as *help me* scrawled on the kitchen wall. Doors lock and unlock on their own; the telephone rings but no one is there and there is no traceable number. These are the prelude to what most people expect of a poltergeist, and that is 'flying objects'.

Before objects 'fly', the first sign that something is very wrong is that things are found to have been moved. Pauline Adams would come down in the morning and discover that furniture had been moved and perhaps an ornament or a plate had been broken. Objects disappearing and reappearing elsewhere is a classic sign that other, more violent, activity is in the wings waiting to explode. It seems almost as if the poltergeist plans the strategy, building up from moving objects to making them disappear altogether. Pauline had been losing shoes: in fact, seven pairs of shoes disappeared over several months. This obviously increases the frustration of the 'victim', making the poltergeist even more malevolent. The electricity supply would switch on and off at random, and Pauline and her mother would smell gas, which would then be 'cured' as soon as it was investigated by the gas board. Pauline even found the money she was saving for a holiday shredded and scattered around. The classic flying objects experience for Pauline and her mother was to have their own crockery hurled at them from out of nowhere as they sat in the lounge. They described being bombarded with china and glassware, which would smash around them as they hurried for cover. They lost all their crockery this way.

This is the prelude to the final stage of a poltergeist's presence, when it can move into possibly harming the occupants by punching and slapping, perhaps holding the victim down, biting them, or making dangerous objects such as knives or other sharp objects fly towards them. Levitation of the victim is also now possible. In the Adams' case, there was a more frenzied level of activity when a young energy was in the house in the form of Mrs Adams' 17-year-old grandson, Stephen. What happened to Stephen has a humorous side to it when described, but was terrifying for him when it occurred.

He was standing in the living room when he felt a force pushing into him. Suddenly, his clothes and shoes flew off him, leaving him standing there in his underpants. His grandma, by now used to shouting at this unseen spirit, asked it to return the clothes, which it did by balancing them on top of the lounge door. Stephen was recorded as saying, 'I had to unbutton all the shirt buttons and unlace the shoes before I could put them on. They had disappeared all buttoned and laced up just as I was wearing them.' Even more bizarre, as soon as Stephen had taken back his clothes, Pauline's missing shoes began dropping one at a time from somewhere above the lounge door. In total, thirteen shoes fell, one shoe never to be returned.

More dangerous moments began to build up for Mrs Adams, her family, and visitors, as objects were now being thrown with more precision. Mrs Adams required stitches after a medicine container struck her on the head. A visiting neighbour had a packet of butter taken out of her basket and thrown at her head. It would only require a sharp object to be hurled for the results to be much more dangerous. When visiting friends decided to photograph an incident in which the figure three from the house number next door had mysteriously planted itself into Mrs Adams' house number 121, turning into 1231, the figure three flew away, striking the photographer on the forehead before the picture could be taken.

The final level associated with poltergeist activity, level 4, can be one in which fires are started, and even sexual offences have been recorded with this degree of closer and closer physical contact between the energy force and its human victims. Blood and threatening messages materializing on walls and floors have all been recorded at this final peak of malevolent activity. Mrs Adams was advised to try and stop it now before all hell broke loose. Case histories across the world show poltergeist activity to be the most reported type of paranormal experience, but, at this level of activity, deaths can result and have done so. Ghostly hauntings do not kill people but poltergeist activity can.

It was now October 1981. The Revd Peter Downham from Greyfriars' church was called in on several occasions. He had a temporary success, but the activities of the poltergeist returned. The cycle can be a continuous one: once level four is reached and survived, it starts all over again from level one.

When *Reading Evening Post* reporter June Wilkinson called to cover the story, she was pursued whilst in the house by a kettle of water and was terrified. Visits and advice from members of the Society for Psychical Research and a medium called Mary Gordon, as well as from another organization, called the Psychic Rescue Group, failed to stop the activities, although the last named did engineer a couple of months' respite. It seemed the only answer was to move, but this entailed the risk of the poltergeist following its source of energy to the new location.

After eighteen months of being plagued by this spirit, they did move to a flat, and, it seems, they were not followed; the activities at number 121 also ceased. Perhaps the cycle is getting ready to start again.

Make sure it was you that left that drawer open and the chair tipped up; you never know.

# BEATEN TO DEATH AT ETON COLLEGE

*Jolly boating weather*
*And a hay harvest breeze.*
*Blade on the feather,*
*Shade of the trees;*
*Swing, swing together,*
*With your bodies between your knees.*

Eton Boating Song, 1863

Eton College – its elite status and vast complex of historic buildings, founded by Henry VI, have made it world famous, but hidden in its past is a tragic episode highlighting a different side to an Eton education. This was the Eton before the start of 'jolly boating weather', the Eton of 1825.

In simple terms, this is the case of two teenage boys who came to blows in their school playground and the sad consequences of that fight. Stated like that, it hardly seems a significant memory of old Eton, but this particular playground fight resulted in two boys facing a charge at Aylesbury Assizes of 'killing and slaying' another.

The victim was the Honorable Ashley Cooper, son of the Earl of Shaftesbury. The boys who were charged were George Alexander Wood, son of Colonel Wood and nephew of the Marquis of Londonderry, and Alexander Wellesley Leith. These were the so-called noble stock of society. This was big news, a scandal that would hardly get a mention if fought by two Berkshire village boys in a dank schoolyard, but here was a chance to glimpse into the closed cloisters of another world, that of the aristocracy.

At this time in the history of Eton College, there was a great deal of scandal of another kind concerning the standard and conditions of teaching at the school. Discipline was a major problem, with the pupils often left to their own devices, especially at night when they were locked in their dormitory. The headmaster was one Dr Keate, whose reputation for flogging the pupils was legendary. He was known also for wearing what could only be described as 'fancy dress, partly resembling the costume of Napoleon, partly that of a widow woman'. It was therefore a school of dubious standards, and Dr Keate's mission, however misinformed to modern eyes, was to bring order and discipline to the boys in his care. He took it upon himself to teach from 100 to 200 boys at any one time, using the spacious upper school as one massive classroom.

On Sunday, 27th February, 1825, around 2 pm in the afternoon, an altercation took place in the school playground between the Hon. Ashley Cooper. and George Alexander Wood. It is not clear what was said, but insults were traded, which soon led to blows between the two boys. Although both lads were nearly fifteen, Wood was much bigger than Cooper. They fought for five minutes or so until the school captain was summoned to deal with them. In the Eton tradition, it was decided that they should meet the following afternoon for an agreed pugilistic contest to settle their differences.

At that time boxing was a sport, with rules laid down in 1743 by one James Broughton. Fights were with bare knuckles, and each round lasted until one fighter was knocked down. The fight ended only when one of the opponents fell to the ground and failed to get up within thirty seconds. Broughton's Rules were tough, but then so was an Eton education. It wouldn't be until 1867 and the introduction of the Queensbury Rules that boxing gloves were brought in, and eventually the twelve-round fight with timed rounds.

On Monday, 28th February, at 4 pm, in front of a large crowd of cheering, jeering and shouting boys, the combatants stripped to the waist and began fighting. The smaller boy, Cooper, was agile, and, shouting that he would never give in, fought hard against the much taller Wood. As Cooper fell and then got up again, the rounds were counted, and when they reached ten, it was clear the younger boy was in considerable trouble. He was weak and exhausted and the noise from the spectators was deafening. Both fighters had boys acting as 'backers' or 'seconds', and they had brought quantities of brandy with them for 'medical assistance'. By the eleventh round, Cooper's 'second', a senior called Alexander Wellesley Leith, poured a large quantity of brandy down Cooper's throat, which did revive him temporarily. However, Cooper was repeatedly struck on the head by Wood, one heavy blow in particular hit his temple and he collapsed in agony. Wood's supporters cheered and proclaimed their man the better, but Cooper was revived once more by Leith, and the fight continued. It had begun at 4 pm and two hours later they were still attempting to fight, both boys exhausted.

Wood, who had had the physical advantage from the start, was not at all badly off compared with Cooper, who was unable to focus or move with any degree of precision. He was in a complete daze. Each time a round was declared, they would both be plied with more brandy. At one point, rather bizzarely, Wood declared he had to attend a tutorial with his tutor Mr Ottery, and so would continue the fight with Cooper later. Cooper's second, Leith, said they should go another round as the fight had not been concluded. He appealed to Cooper's 'backers', one of whom exclaimed, 'We will have another round, we are in no hurry.'

And so they continued. In that round Wood struck a severe blow to Cooper that not only felled him, but Wood also toppled with the exertion and collapsed heavily on top of him. Some reports claim that the boys fought an astonishing sixty rounds before it was finally over for the Hon. Ashley Cooper, who crashed to the ground and lay quite still. Leith now insisted they made up their differences on the spot. Wood lifted Cooper's head, but seeing he was knocked senseless, said nothing and left the scene of the fight with his supporters.

Cooper had two brothers at the college. They picked him up and carried him to the house of the Revd Knapp, where they put

Eton College courtyard

him straight to bed. One of Cooper's brothers stayed by his bedside, but it was four hours before any medical advice was sought. By the time a doctor did arrive, Cooper was dead. The coroner and his jury visited the deceased boy at the Revd Knapps' house on Tuesday, 1st March, at 2 pm. They found his temples, eyes, and the upper part of his cheek bones were jet black with bruises and broken facial bones. His ribs and breast were severely damaged and had obviously been subjected to extreme violence. When the autopsy took place, it was found that he had sustained a rupture of the blood vessels in the brain.

The police were informed, and it was decided that Cooper had been unlawfully killed. Both Wood and Leith were to be indicted for his slaying.

We do not know what Dr Keate had to say about this tragic episode involving his boys, but he had organized some unusual legal arrangements on behalf of George Wood. At a sombre roll call on the morning of Wednesday, 2nd March, the pupils answered to their names in the traditional manner. All were conscious of the fact that one name would never be called again: Ashley Cooper had literally been struck from the register. When Alexander Wellesley Leith's name was called, there was silence. He was absent, and others offered the information that his family had withdrawn him from the college. So Leith, Cooper's enthusiastic second in the fight, had been spirited away. However, when the name of Cooper's opponent was called, George Alexander Wood answered in the affirmative. He was immediately advised that he must consider himself in custody, but special arrangements had been made to keep him from being sent to the county gaol. He was to remain in the college, living at his tutor's house, together with a police officer, who would accompany him at all times. It seems Dr Keate's view was that, as Cooper's death occurred in college grounds in what some might regard as an honorable settlement of differences, the immediate requirements of the law could be accommodated within his jurisdiction.

Cooper's father, the Earl of Shaftesbury, had agreed with this arrangement. His son's funeral was to be that Sunday at the college chapel, so he did not wish to pursue an indictment against George Wood and Alexander Leith at that time but to leave them cited on the coroner's warrant as having unlawfully killed his son. An indictment for manslaughter would follow in due course.

On Wednesday, 9th March, 1825, Wood, aged 14, and Leith, aged 19, appeared at Aylesbury Assizes, charged with the 'killing and slaying' of Cooper. They pleaded not guilty. However, the boys were not alone in the dock. Standing with them as 'friends' were Lord Nugent, Colonel Browne, Colonel Wood, Sir John Dashwood King, the county magistrate, and several other 'gentlemen of distinction'.

In a curious twist of fortune, the three named witnesses for the prosecution were unable to be present at court. We shall never know the precise role played by the 'gentlemen of distinction', but a mysterious and sudden change of heart by the prosecution witnesses meant there was no case to answer. Mr Justice Gaseler ruled, 'There is no prosecution and the prisoners must be discharged.' The two boys bowed to the judge and immediately left the dock with their 'friends'.

Boxing – of the official or the unofficial kind – no longer takes place at Eton College.

# ASCOT'S
# ROYAL ASSASSIN

'*I suffer from arbitrary power*'

Dennis Collins, 1832

The first stone rebounded off the wall, just missing the window. The second, larger and much heavier stone didn't. It went straight through the open window, striking the man inside directly on his forehead and causing him to stagger back and cry, 'Oh! God, I am hit.'

The unknown assailant had been about to hurl a third missile, but he was grabbed by a naval officer, and others nearby rushed to do the same. He was in danger now of being assaulted by an angry crowd but was taken into custody by Bow Street police officers. He was detained and appeared before Sir F.A. Roe, the Chief Magistrate of Westminster, within minutes of the assault. Meanwhile, the victim, hit by a jagged flint-stone, regained his composure and reappeared at the window with his wife, his hat apparently having saved him from the full impact of the assault, although a red swelling had appeared on his forehead.

The missing information that puts this curious tale into context is that the location of the incident was the royal enclosure at Ascot racecourse; the injured man was King William IV; and the date was 19th June, 1832. The race crowd, of course, numbered several thousands, many of whom witnessed the assailant's attack on the king. There were numerous police on duty, and the custom was for the Chief Magistrate of Westminster to be in attendance on all such occasions, just in case. Now that moment had arrived, and he was needed to hold court in a room under the grandstand at Ascot.

Meanwhile, rumours spread rapidly around the racecourse about an assassination plot against the king, the noise of the crowd becoming deafening as their gossip and shouting breached the walls of the improvised court room. The mystery assailant took on different guises according to the rumour. Large, swarthy and ogre-like; a military man from across the seas; a strange foreigner; even a policeman was in the bidding in the crowd's desperate guessing game as to who, why, and how.

Those able to squeeze into the courtroom under the grandstand could not believe their eyes when they saw the man being detained on a committal charge of 'having feloniously and traitorously assaulted our Sovereign Lord the King by throwing a stone with intent to kill his said Majesty'. The penalty for such a crime was certain death, and here before the instant Ascot court stood the plaintiff. He was short, looked very old – at least in his seventies – and was dressed in the tattered garb of a sailor. His most striking feature, however, was a crudely hewn wooden leg. Theories of swarthy foreigners, ogres, and villainous plots were starting to collapse all around. Here was a real mystery: why on earth would such a wretched old man, hindered from escape by a wooden leg, commit such a serious crime?

He was very composed before the assembled crowd, which consisted mainly of those working for the royal family and attached to the royal suite. He chose to say nothing about his attack on the king, only to supply his name, which was Dennis Collins. Was he insane? He did not appear to be so. Moreover, he had walked all the way from London, slept in a shed at Windsor the previous night, and then gone on to Ascot to attack the king. He was committed to Reading gaol for further questioning.

The eager press would have to wait until the following Tuesday to find out the declared motive of one Dennis Collins, would-be assassin of King William IV. Tuesday came, the magistrates came, the press came but Collins did not appear as scheduled at the Wokingham Court. More rumours abounded. Had he escaped? The public wanted to see this mystery assassin. Under orders from Mr Maul, solicitor to the Treasury, he had been kept at Reading

Dennis Collins would have found the present-day racecourse a more difficult place to infiltrate than the Ascot of the 19th century.

gaol and would undergo his hearing there, away from the public view. This fuelled the public imagination even more; he must truly be a dangerous man.

By 2 pm on Wednesday, 27th June, a dozen magistrates or so arrived at the Reading hearing to serve their king and see justice done against the traitor. A substantial part of that afternoon was spent arguing amongst themselves as to who would be the named magistrates on the hearing paper and sign a high treason warrant for committal to Abingdon Assizes: they couldn't all do it.

Once the pecking order was agreed, and the many witnesses again described the stone throwing attack, Dennis Collins was asked what he had to say in his own defence. Was this going to be the final exposure of a long standing conspiracy to assassinate the king, with Collins as the ringleader? With confidence he told the story of how, last December, as an out-pensioner of Greenwich Hospital, he had an argument with the ward keeper, telling him he had no business sweeping the room more than once a day. This led to blows, and Collin's expulsion and the confiscation of his naval pension. As an old, injured sailor, that was all he had to live on. 'I might as well be hanged or shot, as go about starving,' he said. Every attempt he had made since December to restore his right to his pension met with refusal, including his petition to the king himself, on 19th April. The reply from the admiralty was that the king could do nothing for him. 'I suffer from arbitrary power,' he concluded and then apologized for attacking the king. This, however, could not save him from committal to Abingdon Assizes on charges of high treason.

When his trial began on 22nd August, the indictment read that he 'did compass, imagine, devise, and intend the death and destruction of our Lord the king'. This was just the beginning of a long list of charges that referred to his malicious and traitorous intent against the king. The  Attorney General was prosecuting and he reminded the court that 'the prisoner was charged with the highest crime known to the laws of England'.

The prosecution was without complication. Collins was seen in the act of assault: two stones were thrown and a third found in his hand. Witness after witness could testify to the facts of the crime; they were not in dispute. The whole case for the defence had to rest on intent. Did this old pensioner intend to kill His Majesty or cause bodily harm?

Mr Swabey, for the defence, undertook a job of peeling away the persona of an assassin to substitute that of an old serving sailor 'ground down to the soil by poverty'. He went on to say, 'Hunger had deprived him of his reflection and he hazarded his life in the incomprehensible gratification – incomprehensible to the sane mind – of throwing a stone at the king.' The final flourish was to claim his client was *non compos mentis* at the moment he committed the act. The only conspiracy was with himself. The problem for this defence was the fact here was an old man with a home-made wooden leg, who had managed to walk all the way from London to Ascot, arm himself with stones, and proceeded to attack the king. It did not have the element of spontaneity and impulse claimed by Mr Swabey. A second defence lawyer, Mr Carrington, used a different tack, claiming his client had no opportunity of escape or concealment, and the weapon chosen was hardly that of an assassin.

The jury took 15 minutes to find Collins guilty, not of wanting to destroy His Majesty, but to cause him bodily harm. To the jury's obvious dismay and shock, this was to make no difference to the sentence pronounced by Mr Justice Bosanquet, who told Collins 'that you be drawn on a hurdle to the place of execution, and that you be there hanged by the neck till you are dead; that your head be then severed from your body, and your body divided into four parts, to be disposed of as His Majesty shall think proper, and may God Almighty soften your heart and bring you repentance.' The jury did not intend this and immediately signed a petition to spare Collins' life as 'the assault arose from his ignorance'.

Collins languished in Reading gaol awaiting a decision to this surprise appeal for leniency. It came the following year, on Saturday, 16th March, 1833, when a much stouter, fitter, and more colourful 75-year-old Collins appeared before Berkshire Assizes.

*The Devizes & Wiltshire Gazette,* Thursday, March 28th, 1833 reported thus: 'Dennis Collins, the old pensioner who threw a stone at his Majesty, is ordered to be transported for life – so that the poor old man will have the satisfaction of being once more on the element on which he passed so many years of his life. During his confinement at Reading gaol, his personal appearance had undergone considerable alteration. He had become considerably stouter, and his rough, hard looking weather-beaten countenance had assumed a florid complexion and a plumpness, which destroyed much of the marked character of his features. His dress, since his conviction, was most grotesque, all of the right side of it being bright yellow, and all of the left side of a purple brown. His wooden leg (a new one worn for the first time on his trial) was painted sky-blue, and to complete the tout ensemble he wore a blue cloth cap with a red border and a white tassle on top.'

Ascot's one-time assassin died at Port Phillip in Australia in the spring of the following year.

# THE MAN IN THE BLUE SUIT: THE UNSOLVED MURDER OF ALFRED OLIVER OF READING

> '... *every possible link will be followed up in the hope of*
> *bringing this dastardly crime to a successful end.'*
> Chief Inspector Berrett of Scotland Yard, July 17th, 1929

Unsolved murders are much fewer in number than we might imagine. Murder is a crime of such magnitude that inevitably somebody, somewhere at some time is usually apprehended and found responsible (if not always successfully prosecuted). Even when a prosecution is not successful, the police shorthand for indicating their belief that they solved the murder but have been thwarted by the legal system is to issue a press release saying they are not looking for anyone else in connection with the crime. To end up with a brutal murder on their hands and no one even charged, let alone brought to trial, is very rare. It is even rarer when Scotland Yard's equivalents to Sherlock Holmes and his faithful side-kick Dr Watson are brought into the case but it proves to be far from 'elementary my dear Watson'.

It is not giving the game away to reveal to you at this stage that this is probably one of the most frustrating and bizarre unsolved murder investigations on record. This is because our interest lies in why such a seemingly straightforward case still remains such a significant murder mystery. Also, it is still possible, but unlikely, that the murderer is out there somewhere, albeit over 90 years of age, or that someone today knows who it was who murdered 60-year-old Alfred Oliver, purveyor of fine tobacco, in his Cross Street shop on the evening of Saturday, 22nd June, 1929.

One suspect in particular that we will meet appears to have been either an innocent wandering through a string of bizarre coincidences, or a highly devious character capable of a brutal murder. He became the prime suspect, known from witness statements as 'the man in the blue suit'. His name? Philip Yale Drew from Marshfield Hills, Plymouth County, Massachusetts, USA. What really adds the 'stranger than fiction' aspect to this case is that Philip Yale Drew was an actor of some standing, at least in his early stage and movie career in the US. So what brought him to Reading in Berkshire?

Imagine a remote country house with thunder crashing around on a dark and stormy night. Add a mad scientist called Dr Ziska and a beautiful woman trapped in his clutches. To the rescue comes 'Red' Mackenzie, the famous tramp-detective and steely hero of this 90-minute murder melodrama. Enter 49-year-old Philip Yale Drew onto the Reading stage in this highly successful touring production of *The Monster* playing at the Royal County Theatre in Friar Street. But, that same Saturday evening, a few streets away, Alfred Oliver lay dying, viciously bludgeoned for the sake of a few pounds from his till. How were these two events linked, and were Scotland Yard detectives Jim Berrett and Jack Harris clutching at straws in making a connection? You are invited to consider the evidence and draw your own verdict on the man in the blue suit.

Firstly, we need to appreciate that Reading on that Saturday was busy. It was a mecca for those keen on the races at Ascot and Windsor. It was also a gathering place for conmen, thieves, pick-pockets, and race-gangs, all hoping to make a killing of a different kind. The possibility, however, that one of them resorted to murdering Mr Oliver for extra cash cannot be ruled out. The many strangers in town that day provided a 'wild-card' factor that made it almost impossible for the police to detect any one suspicious character.

Imagine such a stranger, up for the races, passing through the throng of Reading, entering Mr Oliver's shop, placing half-a-crown on the counter, asking for cigarettes, and then, as the shopkeeper turned to reach them from the shelf, raining blows on Mr Oliver's head with a heavy weapon. All that remained was to take the money from the till and leave the shop so swiftly and carefully that no one would notice.

The attack on Alfred Oliver, which took place around 6 pm that Saturday evening, whilst his wife Annie was taking the dog for a walk, was not witnessed. There were no cries for help; at least, no one reported as much. He had been sitting comfortably behind the polished shop counter reading about the attractions of Penzance and looking forward to a holiday there with Mrs Oliver the very next week. He was found by Annie slumped behind the counter, blood pouring from his head.

Had he fallen? Was it a heart-attack, she wondered, but he was conscious, thank heaven, and to Annie's concerned cry of 'Olly, my darling, what is the matter?' he was able to mumble, 'I don't know, I don't know.'

Reading police worked hard and fast to deal with this brutal robbery and by 7.30 pm that evening, PC Mogford was able to send the following message to Scotland Yard, to the famous Whitehall 1212 telephone number: 'Attack at 6.15 pm on tobacconist in Cross Street, Reading. Seriously injured by man who entered shop and stole contents of till. At 6 pm two musquash coats and a small brown attaché case containing women's clothes and toilet set stolen from motor car in Broad Street, adjacent Cross Street, by man aged 30 to 40 years, blue suit, clean shaven, very red face, speaks with a Scottish accent. Suspect this man may be assailant of tobacconist. Please circulate description and message.'

Here, from the outset, appears 'the man in the blue suit', with some useful descriptive detail. So far, it is a vicious robbery, which was soon to become a murder inquiry. Indeed, by 11.55 am the following morning, Chief Constable T.A. Burrows also contacted Whitehall 1212 to say, 'Re robbery with violence in Cross Street, Reading. Injured tobacconist now in a critical state. Not expected to live. Please send officer to aid me as soon as possible.' And so it was that the highly successful detective team of Jim Berrett and John Harris travelled from Scotland Yard to Reading Central Police Station in Valpy Street on that Sunday afternoon in June 1929. They were soon at the scene of the crime at number 15

Cross Street. As they arrived, Annie Oliver had returned from the hospital; Alfred Oliver was dead, and a murder inquiry had now officially begun.

In contrast to investigative procedures today, local Police Sergeant Pope had already been to the crime scene and cleaned up all the blood from the floor behind the counter as well as removing the broken tobacco scales, Mr Oliver's shattered glasses, and his broken false teeth. He told Chief Inspector Berrett that there had been no blood on the floor on the public side of the counter, and no apparent blood on the counter itself.

Pope's zealous clean up before the senior detectives arrived seems somewhat counter-productive to the process of detection, but to a great extent detection was an art compared to the scientific approach we are so familiar with today. The powers of forensic science in detecting DNA were still a long way into the future. Detective Sergeant Jim Harris, however, managed to find a bloodstained thumb print on the showcase and splatters of blood where the tobacco, cigarettes, and cigars were displayed. A fingerprint expert and photographer were summoned from Scotland Yard. Zealous as ever, Sergeant Pope also found out that, around the time of the murder, a Mrs Jackson had been barged by a passer-by outside Oliver's shop, someone in a hurry. But, even with Jim Berrett's persuasion, she was reluctant to make a statement. The police knew where she lived and so didn't pursue it further.

Sunday's work was drawing to a close, and Monday promised to be a busy day with the arrival of the fingerprint expert and photographer, who started work immediately. The first task was to go to the Royal Berkshire Hospital to take Alfred Oliver's fingerprints for the purpose of elimination. The two detectives began their pursuit of Mrs Jackson, who still refused to cooperate.

A message from Pangbourne police in the afternoon sent Berrett and Harris swiftly on their way to see a man who claimed he was the murderer. He was nothing more than a drunk, who obviously knew nothing of the crime. By the time they returned to Reading, they found that Sergeant Knight had arrested a 36-year-old local man and charged him with the theft of the musquash coats and other property from the car in Broad Street, but, after questioning, he was eliminated as a murder suspect. It had been a busy day but with little progress for the two detectives. The next day was to see the coroner's inquest in Duke Street.

The atmosphere at the inquest that Tuesday afternoon was emotive.

The coroner, John Lancelot Martin, and many members of the jury knew Mr Oliver: indeed, they were his customers, so it was a very sombre air that pervaded the small courtroom. The proceedings were brief, limited to the legal necessities of indentifying the deceased as Alfred Oliver. It was revealed, however, that in his moments of fleeting consciousness before his death at 5.50 pm on Sunday, 23rd June, he had confirmed to the police that he knew nothing of the attack and just had a memory of reading his book in the shop. The bulk of the discussion that followed was upon the kind of weapon that had been used to inflict such appalling injuries. Suggestions ranged from a coal hammer, a knuckle-duster, to perhaps a jemmy. Whatever it was it was heavy. The court was adjourned for the police to get on with their work and would be reconvened when enough evidence was available to deliver a coroner's verdict.

Now, three days after the murder, came a breakthrough. A local lad, 21-year-old George Jeffries, was in the shop around the time of the murder and he lived only 10 minutes' walk away with his mother at Cherry Court, 36 Castle Street. He told Berrett not only had he entered the shop around 6.08 pm, but he saw the injured shopkeeper lying behind the counter twitching and moaning. Why had he done nothing about it until then? He claimed he had left work as a messenger early to visit his critically ill sister in hospital, and, after dispatching parcels to the post office around 6 pm, he had called in the shop for cigarettes, only to discover the seriously injured Mr Oliver lying on his side, his back to the inside of the counter. Jefferies was unable to see his face when he leant over its polished surface to discover the source of the groaning. He saw blood, became scared, and ran out, still holding his half-crown. He said he did not knock into anyone but just took the parcel receipt book back to his employers and then went straight home.

You are probably thinking the same as Jim Beret did as he looked aghast at this young man. How could he claim to see what he had seen but not report it if he were innocent of the crime? Jefferies' friends Hart and Hendley were also quizzed at the police

## ALARMING OUTRAGE AT A SHOP.

The inquest was opened, yesterday (Tuesday) on the body of Mr. Alfred Oliver, of Reading, a tobacconist, who died on Sunday evening, 24 hours after a brutal attack upon him by an unknown assailant in his shop in Cross-street. So far the theory of the police is that, observing Mrs. Oliver leaving the shop to make a few purchases on Saturday evening about 6 o'clock, the assailant entered the shop, ordered tobacco or cigarettes, and tendered half a crown. While Mr. Oliver was bending over the till to extract change for the half a crown it is thought that he was assaulted. Blows were rained upon his head with a heavy, but sharp, instrument, and he was rendered unconscious. Owing to the fact that the counter does not run the whole length of the shop, but has a flap which permits anyone to get around it, the intruder would find it easy to get to the till, from which Mrs. Oliver states £12 10s. in notes has been extracted.

Mr. Oliver's shop is situated in a narrow thoroughfare between Broad-street and Station-road, and although the street is not frequented by many people on Saturday evening most of the other shops were open, including several grocer's and butchers'. Yet no one appears to have seen the entry or the departure of Mr. Oliver's assailant.

Headline from the *Maidenhead Advertiser* dated 26th June 1929.

station that Wednesday evening in separate rooms and a discrepancy in Jefferies' story emerged. He said he did not have his messenger's bicycle with him during this incident, yet he told his friends he had run out of the shop, leapt on his bike, and made off as fast as he could. Jefferies was allowed to leave the station at around 11.30 pm that evening, with the news his sister had only hours left to live, but he was certainly going to be invited back, decided Berrett. So was he their murderer, this slightly built, pale, thin-featured youth?

Seven days after the terrible attack on Mr Oliver, the two Scotland Yard detectives reviewed their progress. No local shopkeepers had been aware of anything out of the ordinary on that fateful Saturday. However, Mr Foster, the landlord of the nearby Bull in Cross Street, described an encounter with a man about five feet nine inches tall, aged between 30 and 40, unshaven, ruddy complexioned, and having a broad Scottish accent and wearing a blue suit. He knocked on the pub door at around 5.55 pm to see the secretary of the local Scottish Association. He said he needed money, as he was destitute. Mr Foster sent him on his way. With the landlord's description, 'the man in the blue suit' became a focus of media attention.

Other witnesses also told Berrett about such a man. Who was he? Mrs Shepherd put him at around 25-years-old and five feet seven inches, stocky, and wearing a blue suit. He was rushing down Friar Street at about eight minutes past six o'clock. Mr Rivers saw a dark-suited man running down Cross Street itself: he was in his early thirites and about six feet tall. Around 6.05 pm, Mrs Levington was almost bowled over when a tall, fair-haired man shouted, 'Clear out of the way,' and rushed down Broad Street; she didn't mention the suit, however. Berrett's collection of statements continued in similar vein: a man behaving in a peculiar way or with a very red face, and that blue suit again, or perhaps a dark suit rather than blue. Nobody described seeing Jefferies the messenger boy.

Berrett's nose twitched, however, at the very full account given by Alice James, who was walking down Cross Street at around ten minutes past six. She claimed she saw a man standing in the doorway of Mr Oliver's shop. He was tall, with iron-grey hair, around 40 years of age, and she said there was blood splattered on his face, as if he'd been in a fight or perhaps had a nose bleed, but she could not recall what he was wearing. She was unable to pick him out of the Criminal Records Office picture gallery. Nevertheless, Berrett had a gut feeling he was closing in on Alfred Oliver's murderer.

Also, the reluctant Mrs Jackson, previously unable to give Berrett and Harris a statement, had managed to tell the *Daily*

*News* her story and spoke of a man in a dark blue suit and around five feet eight inches tall rushing out of Mr Oliver's shop, colliding with her, shouting 'I'm sorry', and rushing off.

More and more sightings were described, and as well as the suit, the Scottish accent became a regular feature. It seemed only a matter of time before someone would come up with a name.

Leads came and went. It was now Wednesday, 17th July, and Berrett had over 100 witness statements; no weapon had been found; and no man in a blue suit, dark or otherwise, named. Throwing out the chaff, one month's detective work resulted in the following description that Berrett believed was closest to that of the murderer; 'A middle-aged man with iron grey hair, fairly respectable appearance, wearing a dark blue suit and not in the habit of wearing a hat.' (In the 1920s it was unusual to see a man in the street without a cap or hat of some description.) It was not much of a return for over 2,300 pages of case documents. Berrett described the investigation as reaching deadlock.

Most detectives will tell you that then, as much as today, luck played an important part in leading to an arrest. Chief Constable T.A. Burrows was in the Wellington Club in Friar Street, opposite the Royal County Theatre, when a fellow member told him he reckoned that their suspect with the iron-grey hair was one of the actors who had starred in *The Monster* at the time when Mr Oliver was attacked. His name, he confided, was Yale Drew. Burrows decided to follow this lead, and on July 19th telephoned Berrett and Harris, who were now back at Scotland Yard, saying, 'I think we are going to be able to establish the identity of the man whom Mrs James saw in the doorway of Mr Oliver's shop.'

Philip Yale Drew was still pulling in the crowds as the tramp-detective 'Red' Mackenzie, but this time at the Theatre Royal, Nottingham. A letter was drafted to the Chief Constable of Nottingham to arrange a visit from the Reading and Scotland Yard detectives as soon as possible.

Meanwhile, Harris had been pondering over the Jefferies youth and decided to pull him in again and surreptitiously obtain his fingerprints. He learnt from the previously reticent Mrs Jackson that he was not the man who bumped into her, but she did say that a Mrs Luckett had told her how Jefferies had hit his sister over the head with a jemmy at one time. Harris was satisfied that the jemmy incident was gossip, but talked it over with Jefferies, hoping he would place his hands on the table in the interview room, which had been covered with clean white paper. He did so, which meant that by treating this paper with a special black powder they could compare his prints with that bloodstained print on the shop display case. They didn't match.

It was now Wednesday, 22nd July, and a veritable posse of senior police officers representing Scotland Yard, Reading, and Nottingham police gathered together at Nottingham's Guildhall Police Station and decided not to disrupt that evening's performance at the Theatre Royal to speak to the actor. Instead, they had Drew traced to his lodging house at 37 Fox Road, West Bridgeford. Berrett was taking a well-deserved break in Margate; so it was Sergeant Harris, representing Reading's Superintendent Doubleday and Nottingham's Sergeant Ellington who paid Drew a visit at 9.30 am the next day.

Drew was taken aback at his early morning visitors. The reported conversation went as follows. Detective Sergeant John Harris introduced himself and his colleagues and went on to say, 'I am assisting the Chief Constable of Reading and other officers in inquiries respecting a murder which occurred at Reading on Saturday, 22nd June, when I understand you were performing at the County Theatre there, and I would like you to come with me to the police station to be interviewed.'

'Murder?' Drew had gasped, 'What do you want me for? I can't tell you anything. I don't know where I was that day. Are you accusing me?' 'I am accusing no one,' said Harris. 'Will you come to the police station?' Drew agreed, and so begins an episode in his life that totally eclipses any melodrama or whodunit he had been part of on stage or in front of movie cameras.

At the police station, Drew was asked to read and sign a statement, which he did. It said, 'I have been told that I answer the description of a man seen at the scene of the murder and standing in a shop doorway, and have been asked to account for my movements on the day in question. I have been cautioned that what I say will be taken down in writing and may be used in evidence.' Unbeknown to Drew, the same trick with the white paper was in progress during the three hours he was questioned. He maintained his innocence and adopted a rather bewildered

Philip Drew as 'Red' Mackenzie, in the touring production of *The Monster*. The woman is his manageress Marion Lindo acting under her stage name of Marion Wakeford. (© Thames Valley Police Force Museum)

attitude throughout, denying he'd ever been near Cross Street in Reading, let alone any tobacconist shop. Disappointingly for the police, it was not his thumb-print found on the showcase.

The local and daily press loved it. Here was a well-known actor, idolized and adored by thousands of fans, now embroiled in a real-life murder case whilst also playing a detective on stage.

On Friday, he was called back to Guildhall police station, and it was a different man who entered the interview room. He was stressed and upset, the whole ordeal was affecting him and his work as an actor: he protested, he cried. Whilst he was being questioned, another police officer was following up a lead to a local cleaning firm to recover clothes Drew had left for cleaning. He was successful in procuring Drew's blue suit jacket from the cleaning firm and it was sent down to London for examination. Meanwhile, Drew was free to go.

His next encounter with the police was on August 7th, in St Albans. The production had moved towns, and Drew struggled on under the immense strain of police surveillance as the theatrical tour continued to honour its booking commitments. Again he signed cautions and was interrogated for over three hours. He was stressed and drinking heavily. His jacket had revealed no blood stains, only signs of recent chemical cleaning. He had not been able to produce the blue matching trousers, which he claimed had mysteriously disappeared on the day of the attack on Mr Oliver. He'd claimed he'd packed them in his trunk in his Reading dressing room on the day in question, but when he got to Maidstone, the next town on the tour, they were not there. Drew was allowed to go.

Two days later, on April 9th, lo and behold, his blue serge trousers mysteriously re-appeared in his dressing room at St Albans, draped across his trunk. Drew told the police, who took them for examination. They revealed nothing, but Berrett was very suspicious of Drew and of his habit of not being able to recall his movements on the day in question when it appeared to suit him.

We need to remind ourselves that Drew had not been arrested or charged, but was merely helping police with their inquiries. The ordeal was taking its toll on his health and stamina. Whilst Drew continued to tour the country as 'Red' Mackenzie, the date was decided for Alfred Oliver's inquest to reconvene. It was to be Wednesday, October 2nd, and Drew was promised star billing. He decided to play the celebrity card and booked himself into the Great Western Hotel, Reading on October 1st in readiness for the following day's performance in the coroner's court.

The inquest opened at 11.25 am and it promised to be a detailed and prolonged affair. Berret and Harris had many witnesses up their sleeve, whom they knew were likely to identify Philip Yale Drew as the man in the blue suit.

After covering the details of Mr Oliver's discovery by his wife and the details of what had happened to the poor man, it was the messenger, George Jefferies, who was called to be questioned. He still could not explain why he had not come forward immediately he discovered the injured tobacconist, maintaining he was 'scared to death'. When the story made the paper, he was frightened to come forward and worried he'd lose his job. He was also distressed by the fact that his sister was in hospital dying. His friends had advised him to tell the police and they thought he'd used his bike when he hadn't; so it all became too confusing for him to deal with. He was allowed to step down.

Unexpectedly, it was the local butcher, Mr Loxton, who caused a stir.

He told the story of an eccentric man, who could have been Irish, Scottish, or even American, who had been in his shop, which was located next door but one to Mr Oliver's shop. It was around 1.30 pm on Saturday, 22nd June, and this man had asked, 'Have you got any liver?' but left before Mr Loxton could reply. The butcher then saw him again, between 5.30 and 6 pm looking in the wireless shop opposite the tobacconist's. He started to walk away, looking agitated, and then headed towards Mr Oliver's shop and out of view. He then described a man about 5 feet 8 inches tall, clean shaven, with a sallow face, no hat, and long dark hair that was in a rough state. He was wearing a navy-blue suit, brown shoes, and a collar and tie. Asked by the coroner if anyone in the court resembled that man, he confirmed there was such a person, 'That gentleman sitting there,' and he pointed to Philip Yale Drew. The coroner asked Drew to stand and Mr Loxton to be absolutely certain it was the same man. Drew stood and Loxton swore on oath that he was the man he had seen.

The atmosphere was electric. Drew, who had always denied to Berrett and Harris any knowledge of being in Cross Street, had been placed at the scene of the crime in a court of law, albeit an inquest and not a criminal trial. The inquest was adjourned until the next day at 11 am, and Drew was advised by a friend that it might be appropriate for him to secure a solicitor, which he did: one Frederick James Ratcliffe.

Berrett and Harris's star witness, Mrs Alice James, began the second day with her description of the man with iron-grey hair, apparently wiping blood from his face as he stood in the Oliver's shop doorway. She had noticed the town hall clock at ten minutes past six. Again the coroner asked if such a person was present in the court, and, without hesitation, Mrs James identified Drew. Drew's newly appointed solicitor questioned whether she really did see Drew and whether she really saw him with blood on his face. She would not be swayed. He was trying to hide an injury or wipe an injury and he wore a dark blue suit, and it was Philip Yale Drew.

As the witnesses came forward, one after the other, one could be forgiven for forgetting it was an inquest rather than a murder trial and that Drew was an invited participant rather than a prisoner in the dock. Witness after witness placed him in and around Cross Street, somewhere he had told Detective Harris he'd never visited when he was interrogated in Nottingham in July. They described this man with iron-grey or unruly hair, full-faced, thick set, aged 40 to 50, and wearing a blue suit, with a mac draped over his shoulder like a cape. He was behaving eccentrically, gazing at Cross Street shops, stroking a car, appearing to stroke or measure a lamp post close to Oliver's shop, walking in the middle of the road, staggering, muttering, and generally behaving in a drunken manner. Six witnesses were positive it was him, placing him at Cross street at various times throughout the day leading up to Alice James's account. Another witness said he only resembled the man he saw, and one witness, who described the man stroking the lamp post, could not identify Drew in the courtroom.

Two other witness described how they had met with Drew the day before the attack on Oliver. Herbert Booth accompanied him to the Welcome Café in Cross Street for eggs and bacon around 10.30 am that Friday morning, and Reginald Barber had shaved Drew around 1.45 pm on the same day. Before the coroner, both identified Drew as the man.

A crucial question, however, had not been answered: if the man in Oliver's shop doorway seen by Mrs James at around 6.11 pm was not Drew, who was it, and where was Drew at that time? It was on the third day of the inquest, 4th October, that there arose an important three-way conflict of evidence concerning Drew's whereabouts at that significant time, just before and just after 6 pm.

According to Alfred Fry, the stage manager for the production of *The Monster*, he heard Drew singing as he entered the stage door at around 6 pm but did not see him. He then saw him at 6.15 or 6.17 pm outside his dressing room in his stage clothes and a little drunk, with half-completed make-up. Mrs Goodhall, Drew's landlady at his lodgings in nearby King's Meadow Road, said Drew had rushed out the house around 6.10 pm, which meant Fry couldn't have heard him singing at 6 pm by the stage door. In the past, Drew had told Mrs Goodhall he could be from her sitting room and on the stage in seven minutes flat. He would often run to the theatre, muttering to himself and inebriated. Mrs Goodhall's evidence was independently supported by two neighbours, Mrs Crouch and Mrs Green, who both saw him rushing off from King's Meadow Road towards the theatre at around 6 or 6.10 pm.

Finally Bertie Hathaway described the familiar, blue-suited Drew, raincoat slung across his shoulders, in Friar Street around 6.14 pm, muttering and rushing drunkenly into the stage door entrance to the Royal County Theatre.

This now casts doubt on who exactly Mrs James saw in the doorway of Oliver's shop at 6.11 pm, and she was the only witness to make this observation. But are the times accurate? Drew's landlady admitted the clocks in her house were not that reliable; but we then have the other ladies who support the time he rushed out of his lodgings at 9 King's Meadow Road. The police had already timed a normal walk from Mrs Goodhall's house to Oliver's shop as taking four minutes 45 seconds. From there to the theatre took two minutes 20 seconds, a total of seven minutes five seconds at a moderate walk. Was there a timing solution that meant Drew could have run to Oliver's, committed the crime, and then got to the theatre to be seen in stage costume and part make-up by 6.17 pm? It was possible, but not if Drew was in King's Meadow Road at 6.10 pm; if it was nearer 6 pm, or just a few minutes after, it would be feasible.

As the inquest dragged on, *The Monster* touring company was now in danger of disbanding and Drew, although bolstered by the many fans waiting to glimpse him outside his hotel and the courtroom, was feeling distinctly depressed and drinking heavily with the strain of being on trial, yet not being on trial. His solicitor advised Drew he was appointing a barrister, William Arthur Fearnley-Whittingstall, to see the rest of the inquest through.

The increased media attention and slow build-up to what could result in a murder charge against Drew meant that when day four of the inquest was about to start on Monday, October 7th, crowds were beginning to build until the route from the Great Western Hotel to the Valpy Street court were crowded by thousands of people: the curious, of course, but lots of well-wishers and fans.

That morning saw a new development. Drew's missing blue trouser story was relayed to the court and the observation made that new pockets had recently been sewed into them. Was this done during their 'missing period' to eliminate blood stains? Had his jacket gone to the Nottingham cleaners for the same reason? Why had Drew denied knowing about Cross Street when he had been in the café there eating eggs and bacon with Herbert Booth on the Friday, and then on the Saturday afternoon had apparently called into Loxton's Cross Street butcher's shop to ask about liver?

The inquest took the direction of analysing Drew's character. Was he a violent man? Was he an honest man? The fans had no doubt he was honest, innocent, and a gentleman, but they were not giving evidence. Drew took the stand on Tuesday, October 8th, on the advice of his counsel. His actor's confidence and poise had returned, but stood out in stark contrast to his answers concerning his movements on the day and evening of Oliver's murder: they were vague, hesitant, and somewhat rambling.

After an hour and 20 minutes in the witness box, it was clear that, although Drew could remember his lines on stage, his memory for where he was on the day in question was, to use his own description, 'erratic'.

Was he the man in the blue suit behaving strangely in Cross Street and finally seen leaving Oliver's shop doorway around the time of the murder? Drew provided no answers precise enough to take him out of this time frame or location, whereas many other witnesses had sworn to have seen him around the murder scene.

The foreman of the inquest jury, frustrated at Drew's performance, went so far as to say to him, 'As you cannot give any explanation of your movements on Saturday, June 22nd, before arriving at the theatre, do you suggest that the sworn testimony of the witnesses as to your movements in regard to Cross Street and to the theatre is perjury?' True to form Drew replied, '... there are so many witnesses against me, with so many different accounts of time, I'm afraid I would not like to say they had committed perjury.' It was true, the weight of witness evidence pointed the finger at Drew, and it seemed that he was now closer to facing a verdict that would take him to a criminal trial for the wilful murder of Alfred Oliver. Except there was another witness, who would prove to be pivotal for Drew's future freedom.

This witness had given a statement to the police concerning a man in a blue suit at the scene of the crime, but had not been called to give evidence. In fact the police had mislaid his statement and he was not on the witness list, an omission noticed by Bernard O'Donnell, a crime reporter for the *Empire News*, who was aware of how important this witness was to Drew's case. Alfred John Wells, a local butcher, was tracked down by this enterprising reporter, who had become a friend to Drew, believing in his innocence, and rushed to take the stand. Cross-examined by Mr Fearnley-Whittingstall, Wells, in contrast to Drew, was a clear and precise witness. He both saw and spoke to a man in a blue suit in the Welcome Café at 7.30 am on the day in question, a man who had a habit of wiping his hand across his face in the manner of the man seen by Mrs James in Oliver's shop doorway. Again, around 5.40 pm that evening, in the Cross Street area, he saw the same man two or three times, a mac slung over his shoulder.

Wells' original statement was located and rushed to the inquest. It showed Wells had gone to the police station on the night of the murder and given a precise description of the man in the blue suit at the scene of the crime, a description he recalled in exactly the same detail in court and before the last-minute location of his mislaid statement.

The atmosphere was one of tangible anticipation as Drew's QC, Fearnley-Whittingstall, addressed Wells and asked, 'Would you recognize him again?' Drew was asked to stand up; Wells replied 'That is not the man.' This simple reply totally reversed the

Philip Yale Drew (centre) on his way to hear the verdict of the coroner's court. He is supported by his manageress Marion Lindo and her husband, Frank. (© Thames Valley Police Museum)

proceedings. Wells also added that his man in the blue suit had a North Country accent. Drew left the court that afternoon, a weight lifted from his shoulders and adoring fans scrambling to see and touch him, but it was not over yet: the verdict was to be the next day.

The scene for the finale was as expected: crowds clapping and cheering, and the police struggling to hold them back as Drew entered the town hall for the coroner's summing up and the jury's verdict. Over 60 witness had given evidence, and the coroner recounted to the jury the flavour of that evidence and the doubts that still existed over the timing of the murder and the movements and identity of the man in the blue suit. The jury retired.

An hour went by and the anticipation was palpable. Outside

was gridlock, with people standing on the roofs of their cars to try and see what was happening inside the town hall. Another hour and a half slowly ticked by, then things began to move: the jury was returning. The foreman stood, their verdict written on the paper clutched in his hand. He was asked to read it slowly. He did so: 'Mr Coroner, the jury have, after very careful deliberation on all the evidence submitted to them, unanimously agreed that the evidence is too conflicting for them to definitely establish the guilt of any particular person, consequently they return a verdict of wilful murder against some person or persons unknown.'

The inquest was over and the crowds went wild. The people of Reading had taken to Drew, and now, just like a theatrical adventure, the hero had survived, and celebrations would continue for Drew's entourage and fans alike. But who did murder Alfred Oliver? Were there two men in blue suits in and around the area – both rather eccentric – one an American actor, innocently blundering about, worse the wear from drink, and another, a North Country man stroking cars and lamp-posts and with a habit of wiping his face as if removing blood?

The crime was unsolved. For Drew, the post-inquest publicity, both good and bad, continued. He was desperate for the police to find a new suspect as his life went rapidly downhill and his career lay in ruins. He wrote, 'I have nothing more in worldly possessions than the clothes I wear. I have no money; I have no work, simply and solely because I am Philip Yale Drew, the actor who was a witness before the coroner in the Reading murder.'

'Why,' he wanted to know, 'have I received no compensation for my mutilated blue suit?'

The mystery of the man in the blue suit remains on file.

# THE NIGHT LAMBOURN
# WAS SET ON FIRE

Wander through the churchyard of the ancient parish church of St Michael and All Angels in the historic village of Lambourn and you'll discover a curious tombstone, a tombstone with a message.

John Carter lies beneath it, the last man in England to be executed for arson, convicted of setting fire to his home village of Lambourn.

Over 5,000 people witnessed his death on the scaffold at the top of Reading gaol on 16th March, 1833, a spectacle designed both to entertain and deter. As a deterrent, the message was carried over to his grave. But did this young man really request his death be used as a warning 'to his companions and others?' Who might these 'others' be, and who were his 'companions'? This message may have come from this young married man, who had two infants and worked as a general labourer in Lambourn, but it is very unlikely. This is more likely a dire warning from the governing bodies of Lambourn and elsewhere, including London. It contains the ultimate health warning to other labourers who were felt to be engaging in plots that extended beyond the mere physical boundaries of Lambourn. Indeed, in sentencing Carter to death, the judge claimed it was a long premeditated scheme on the part of Carter to throw the country into a state of alarm and panic.

What was going on at this time that led the *Berkshire Chronicle* of 1832 to apologize to its readers for not being able to fully report

Here
lies the body
of John Carter
of this parish, labourer,
who in defiance of the laws
of God and man,
wilfully and maliciously
set fire in two places
to the town of Lambourn
on the 19th November 1832
And was executed at Reading
in the 30th year of his age
on the 16th day of March, 1833,
having desired that his body
might be interred here as
a warning to his companions
and others who may hereafter
read this memorial of his
untimely end.
The wages of sin is death.
Repent and
turn yourselves from
all your transgressions and so iniquity
shall not be your ruin.

The inscription on John Carter's tombstone which can be found in the churchyard at Lambourn.

on the fires at Lambourn 'in the interests of justice'? Who were the London strangers asking questions in the town about the labouring men working there? And how could a mere unemployed agricultural labourer throw the country into such a state of alarm and panic?

The destruction caused by fire can be devastating at any time, but in a place full of thatched cottages, stables, and wooden barns packed with straw, it is particularly disastrous. On the evening of

19th November, 1832, at about 7.30 pm, two fires broke out at almost the same moment, one at the Red Lion Inn in the centre of Lambourn and the other at Mr Spicer's Malthouse Barn, about 400 yards distant. The flames shot up in an instant and, at the Red Lion, killed valuable horses and a sporting dog in the stables.

There had been a coursing meeting that day and the animals' owners were dining at the inn. The other fire, at Spicer's barn near Crowel Corner, was about to reach the adjoining outhouse stacked up to 15 feet high with straw. Several passers-by alerted others, the church bells were rung, and everyone, including John Carter, rushed to fight the blaze that threatened to destroy everything. It was agreed by all that if the night had not been calm, damp, and misty, the whole place would have been burnt down.

George Green, a labourer who lived in a part of Lambourn known as 'the city', had been passing Crowel Corner that evening and had seen John Carter reach his hand into the thatch of the outhouse and shamble away; 30 minutes later the blaze was visible. Green challenged Carter and said to him, 'John this is a bad job.' Carter said the fire shouldn't have broken out for another two hours, at which Green replied, 'For God's sake John hold thy tongue.' Carter replied, 'So I will,' and they both joined in the battle to save Lambourn from destruction.

Another labouring acquaintance of Carter, Robert Chivers, was also fighting the fire, a fire he knew would happen. Only hours before, he had been given a cloth packet containing a crude incendiary device, with an agreed plan that whilst Carter set fire to the Red Lion and Mr Spicer's premises Chivers would set a third fire going in Mr Child's pigeon house, about 220 yards away. This would have certainly sealed Lambourn's fate, but a pang of conscience led Chivers to throw his device away.

Mr Child, who lived in the Malthouse, paid Chivers, Carter, and other labourers who assisted in fighting the fires that night well for their hard work in saving Lambourn from destruction. This was a strange irony, since it was said that the firing was a plot to raise labourers' wages. According to Chivers, Carter had said to him that he did not think there would be better times at Lambourn until there was a good fire.

Similar fires at Bedwyn in Wiltshire gave credence to theories of plotting and this is explains the presence of London strangers in

Crowel Corner in Lambourn, where John Carter left an incendiary device in the roof of Spicer's Barn.

Lambourn following the fire. These were Bow-Street detectives, known simply as Ruthven and Stevens, who were working undercover, with instructions to leave no stone unturned. Somewhere in Lambourn there was said to be a man who made incendiary devices, known simply as 'making a match'.

It was the curiosity of Mrs Pheobe Hall which provided this crucial evidence, when, at about 8.45 am on the morning after the fire, she saw something on the ground opposite Mr Gearing's brewhouse which she said 'looked like a poultice off someone's thumb'. She handed it in to Mr Spicer, who took it to the Revd Hippisley, who handed it to Ruthven. It was the incendiary device made by Carter and discarded by Chivers.

With the assistance of a Lambourn magistrate, the Revd Hippisley, Ruthven, and Stevens successfully apprehended eight labourers in Lambourn and at least four in Wiltshire.

Of the eight detained in Lambourn, three were taken to trial, and others, tempted by a reward or immunity from prosecution, gave evidence against them. The indictment ran to ten counts, and John Carter was charged with the plotting, planning and manufacture of incendiary devices, and with committing arson. Henry Rider and William Winkworth were indicted as accessories 'before the crime was committed'.

Rider had apparently said to Carter that he'd give him a quart of beer for a good fire, whilst Winkworth was claimed to have commented that he would have set the Malthouse on fire if he lived as near to it as Carter. Chivers had become the main prosecution witness against Carter. There were no defence witnesses.

Rider and Winkworth were acquitted and Carter alone found guilty. Carter had hoped for a sentence of transportation, commenting he was looking forward to a new life across the sea, but the judge had other ideas. He was of the opinion that those acquitted were just as guilty and that they needed 'a lesson for the future'. That lesson was to be Carter's execution. Carter claimed that others he wouldn't name had drawn him into this and that there was a Lambourn man, a mystery match-maker, who was never identified.

Just as the trapdoor opened and John Carter dropped to his death at the end of a rope at noon on 16th March, a mystery arsonist struck, firing the extensive fir plantation at Mortimer, eight miles south of the Reading scaffold. No one was apprehended, but I suspect they got the message. After all, it was carved in stone.

# A BRIEF MOMENT
# OF TIME

*'Time present and time past,*
*Are both perhaps present in time future,*
*And time future contained in time past.'*
T.S. Eliot, Burnt Norton, *Four Quartets*,1935

The concept of time contains much mystery and intrigue and Eliot's famous poem from his collection entitled *Four Quartets* sets us all a challenge. How far are we able to grasp and understand those fleeting moments of sudden illumination and apparent perception that appear to bring past, present, and future together? These cyclical patterns of time can be so varied. There are moments when we are all likely to see our parents in ourselves, saying things that we realize sound like our mother or father or some other relative, and we recall how we had, in the past, vowed never to do so. Past, present, and a hint of the future combine in that brief moment. We shake it off and re-pledge to try not to repeat it, perhaps recalling the sayings, habits, or gestures that so irritated us and gave rise to that pledge in the first place. Heaven forbid, I sound just like my – !

The most common experience regarding time and its complexities is that of déjà vu, literally translated as 'already seen'. It's that confusing moment when you know you've been in that same situation before, you know what you will say and you know what those around you will say, and it seems as if all has been rehearsed before.

Over 70 percent of the population admit to such experiences, and it is much higher amongst mid-teen to mid 20-year-olds.

Even Freud regarded the déja vu experience as 'in the category of the miraculous'. Contemporary theorists are less enthusiastic and put it down to a simple fantasy or perhaps wish fulfillment, but parapsychologists hold to their belief that it is a fleeting glimpse of a past time, even a past life.

One Swiss scholar, Arthur Funkhouser, divided this experience of déjà vu into two types: one is *déjà visite* which means 'already visited' and the other is *déjà vecu*, meaning 'already experienced or lived through'.

A recent Berkshire tale experienced by Jeff and Amanda seems to take on these experiences and even add yet another time-related phenomenon known as a *timeslip*. For example, there is an everyday form of timeslip that most car drivers have experienced: that of reaching a familiar place, perhaps reaching your house, suddenly to realize that you cannot recall much of the drive itself. Bits of the driving experience are missing. There is a gap in time. The moment passes, but you assume that you were on some kind of autopilot, which is probably correct; nevertheless, it's a little unsettling. Well, for Jeff and Amanda, the mystery of their time-slip experience in October 1993 has left them puzzled and perplexed to this day.

They had set off for an evening out at the Crown pub in Marlow. This was their regular haunt, where they met up with their friends most weekends. Jeff always took the same route. He'd drive over from Wraysbury to collect Amanda from her home just outside Slough. It was a dry October night and they were looking forward to a Friday night session in the Crown. From Amanda's house they would take the route via Maidenhead, travelling along the A4094 and following the river down past Cookham. This took them through Bourne End and on to Marlow.

They chatted about a birthday celebration that was going to be held the very next evening. This was for Jeff's friend Jason, and he was having his birthday bash in the Cookham Tandoori, which is just off Cookham High Street. Amanda had agreed to be the driver the following night and wanted to know precisely where the

A view of the route along the A4094, where the Cookham Tandoori is located.

restaurant was located. As they were going to pass by the road leading to the restaurant on their way to the Crown, Jeff slowed down in order to point it out. They approached Cookham High Street to their left as usual and he slowed right down and pointed along the road to show Amanda where the restaurant was located. Jeff then resumed normal speed and carried on towards Marlow along the A4094.

They passed one of their usual landmarks, the Ferry Pub; then, after approximately another quarter of a mile, Jeff noticed something very odd indeed. He was approaching Cookham again. They were back in time to that same moment of approaching Cookham High Street and passing by the spot where only minutes before he'd pointed out the location of Cookham Tandori to Amanda. It was *déjà visité* and *déjà vecu*.

Jeff said nothing initially, then Amanda confirmed that despite travelling in a straight line, passing by Cookham High Street, and on past the Ferry to Marlow, somehow they were momentarily jerked back in time to an earlier, but significant, point of their journey. It was not possible to accidently loop back on this route;

it was matter of passing straight through and on to Marlow.

It was hardly a life-threatening experience; it was not particularly traumatic, but it was, they both agreed, very spooky. Jeff recalled, 'It scared the hell out of us and will stay with me for the rest of my life.'

It seems likely that they had come across one of the rarer forms of timeslip. Most timeslips find the participant entering a shop, or area, or location of some kind that has momentarily slipped back to its earlier incarnation, perhaps Edwardian, Victorian, or much much earlier. Then suddenly it returns to the present day scene. Or perhaps the quaint hotel you stayed at actually does not exist when you try to re-book a return visit. You find it had been demolished many years before your visit actually took place!

Jeff and Amanda's form of timeslip, creating an almost instant déjà vu, is less dramatic but more interesting for the parapsychologists. They describe a timeslip as 'a perceived fold or bridge in time that brings the present in contact with another time'. The vast majority of such timeslips, however brief and however ordinary, construct a link with the past, and some provide a bridge to a future view.

Did Jeff and Amanda travel back, albeit briefly, through time? They think so, and it certainly made Jason's birthday the next evening at Cookham Tandori one they would never forget driving to.